Seeking Excellence
Through Independence

Seeking Excellence Through Independence

Liberating Colleges and Universities from Excessive Regulation

Terrence J. MacTaggart and Associates

Jossey-Bass Publishers • San Francisco

Substantial discounts on bulk quantities of Jossey-Bass books are available to corporations, professional associations, and other organizations. For details and discount information, contact the special sales department at Jossey-Bass Inc., Publishers (415) 433–1740; Fax (800) 605–2665.

For sales outside the United States, please contact your local Simon & Schuster International Office.

Jossey-Bass Web address: http://www.josseybass.com

Manufactured in the United States of America using Lyons Falls D'Anthology paper, which is a special blend of non-tree fibers and totally chlorine-free wood pulp.

Library of Congress Cataloging-in-Publication Data

MacTaggart, Terrence J.
    Seeking excellence through independence : liberating colleges and universities from excessive regulation / Terrence J. MacTaggart and associates.—1st ed.
        p.   cm.—(The Jossey-Bass higher and adult education series)
    Includes bibliographical references (p.) and index.
    ISBN 0-7879-0922-X (alk. paper)
    1. University autonomy—United States. 2. Public universities and colleges—United States. 3. Higher education and state—United States. I. Title. II. Series.
LB2331.4.M33   1998
378' .05' 0973—dc21   97-48664

FIRST EDITION
HB Printing   10 9 8 7 6 5 4 3 2 1

The Jossey-Bass
Higher and Adult Education Series

Contents

Preface

It is time to liberate public colleges and universities from excessive regulation if they are to be strong, vital institutions that give first-rate service to the public. The problems facing public higher education in the United States are serious. Public treasuries lack resources, and the public itself may lack the inclination to continue to support the enterprise at current levels, much less pay for the rising tide of new students clamoring for service in the western and southern states. Yet hope for access to high-quality, relevant educational programs matches concern that spaces in college will be in short supply or priced beyond the reach of many Americans. At the same time, university leaders find themselves gridlocked between, on the one hand, the forces of convention, faculty senates and unions, and the whole weight of academic tradition, invested in familiar educational practices that have worked well in the past and, on the other hand, governors, legislators, and opinion leaders across the political spectrum insisting on dramatic, if undefined, change. One alluring response to this dilemma is to intensify the command-and-control philosophy, which sees tighter, more centralized, and authoritarian regulation of public higher education, often under the suzerainty of the state executive branch, as the best way to ensure access, efficiency, and quality. The other alternative, which this book recommends, is to free up colleges and universities, and the systems of these institutions, from excessive regulation in order to capture the benefits of independence. This book has been written to help leaders understand and implement independence in ways that truly revitalize institutions *and* guarantee the bona fide public interest in quality and access.

Policymakers, academics, and advocates of reform are engaged in a lively debate over the merits of centralization versus autonomy when it comes to serving the public interest. Proponents of a strong hand for state control through coordinating boards and agencies argue that they meet public goals by reducing program and administrative duplication, insulating campuses from political intrusion, and keeping the focus on state priorities. Champions of greater institutional freedom assert that such bureaucratic oversight reduces students' ability to choose among truly distinctive options, stifles leadership and creativity at the campus level, increases costs, and substitutes one brand of intrusion for another. With liberalization of national economies, reductions of trade barriers, and privatization of government services racing across the globe as countries struggle to compete internationally (Slaughter and Leslie, 1997), interest in deregulating higher education can only increase in the United States as well.

The outcome of this debate has enormous implications for all stakeholders. Will a free-market approach to higher education cost less, produce higher levels of quality, and still guarantee a generous degree of access, or will a new autonomy sprout more high-cost, elitist "public Ivys," encourage overinvestment in graduate programs and highly specialized research, and fortify the reluctance to teach ordinary undergraduate students? How much deregulation can we afford without sacrificing legitimate public interests? For example, should the new autonomy be restricted to procedural or administrative matters, as Robert Berdahl suggests in this book, or is a more fully privatized scheme, advocated by Kenneth Shaw, the best way to ensure vital, creative college and university leadership? Should the free-market model as practiced in Michigan be adopted by other states, or is more oversight required to reconcile the aspirations of colleges and universities with the priorities of taxpayers and their representatives? Do deregulation and privatization threaten the grand idea of public higher education as a public good, or has the ideal of a government's providing education as a common good so eroded that privatization has become inevitable? Will strategies to make public institutions act more like private ones accelerate public disinvestment?

This book examines the arguments for and against freeing up public colleges and universities not from an ideological viewpoint but in terms of what seems to work and what does not. A clear look at what actually occurs in less regulated environments, for example, indicates that greater competition does not reduce costs, as some proponents suggest. At the same time, the argument that system and coordinating boards insulate campuses from political intrusion, as the experience of New Jersey illustrates, is not universally true.

In the future, will proponents of autonomy and deregulation carry the day, or will a countertrend toward more authoritarian methods prevail? The outcome of this struggle is uncertain. Attempts to expand independence include the ongoing experiment in New Jersey; the creation of charter universities in Maryland and South Carolina; granting exemptions to some regulations for one state university within a system in Minnesota; attempts to dispense with the regulatory burden of state agencies from Oregon to Wisconsin to New York and Connecticut, and elsewhere; the elimination of two governing boards in Illinois; and concerted efforts to decentralize within systems in California, Maine, and elsewhere. There are probably more examples of states' taking steps to concentrate authority in fewer hands at more senior levels, often tied closely to the executive branch of state government. Centralizing and decentralizing initiatives often occur simultaneously. For example, restructuring in Minnesota tightened the control of state agencies over four-year and two-year colleges at the same time that one institution, Winona State University, received modest exemptions from some state regulation.

After studying the centralizing trends in several states, a group of associates and I concluded that attempts to improve performance or efficiency through greater centralized control typically do not work. The sheer complexity of trying to harness more than sixty campuses into one system in Minnesota, the difficulty of shepherding a politically sensitive bill through a contentious state legislature in Maryland, the burden of keeping politics out of organizational change in Massachusetts, and flawed execution of restructuring in Alaska continue to trouble public higher education in these states. In contrast, restructuring and greater centralization are succeeding in North Dakota because gifted leaders carefully planned change on a manageable scale (MacTaggart and Associates, 1996).

This book contributes to the sometimes hot debate over the choice between relatively autonomous institutions and oligarchic control in several ways. It presents and clarifies the key terms, concepts, and arguments that have been generously tossed about. It examines in various levels of detail specific cases and practices that illustrate how greater autonomy seems to be working. Full chapters are devoted to Michigan, where a tradition of university independence has prevailed since before statehood; New Jersey, where the state colleges became largely self-governing in 1994; and Maryland, where St. Mary's College is ably succeeding under a special charter with the state. The chapter authors suggest practical changes in the way presidents lead, boards oversee, and power is sorted out among colleges and universities, coordinating boards, and state executives in order to take advantage of the energies released by greater autonomy. One chapter evaluates the role of technology on organizational structure. The final chapter offers policy options for boards and states wishing to pursue the benefits that independence offers.

Audience for This Book

This book addresses the interests of practitioners within higher education: trustees, chancellors, presidents, administrators at all levels, faculty and student leaders, and others concerned with the future of this enterprise. Governors, legislative leaders, and those with special responsibilities for educational and regulatory policy and their staffs will find the issues, examples, and recommendations offered here useful in their work. Other policymakers and regulators—whether they work under the auspices of coordinating or governing boards or within state agencies such as an attorney general's office or departments of finance, personnel, or administration—may disagree with some of the views expressed in this book, but they will be challenged by the arguments. Although written primarily for practitioners, this book also offers ideas of interest to students of higher education, as well as scholars in the areas of governance and state relations.

Organization of the Book

Part One suggests why the time is right to deregulate public higher education. In the initial chapter, I define the key concepts in the debate over deregulation, then summarize and critique the arguments favoring liberalization. The most compelling reasons to endorse deregulation, I conclude, are to preserve the basic academic freedom to teach, conduct research, and communicate ideas without interference from political or ideological interests and to encourage more creative leadership at the campus level. These views are based on findings of other authors, as well as my own experience as a campus and system chief executive.

Bold and often unbelievable claims are made for information technology as the agent of either Orwellian central domination or radical independence. James Mingle and Rhonda Martin Epper in Chapter Two take a sober look at how technology is actually being used and conclude that electronic communications can contribute to centralization and the reverse, and will likely result in other dramatic changes in power. For example, the high capital costs of technology and fear of competition from entrepreneurs specializing in technologically delivered distance education will compel conventional institutions to collaborate if they are to compete successfully. Mingle and Epper conclude that as educational services become increasingly available over the Internet, the locus of power in higher education will shift from state bureaucrats, systems, and institutions to consumers themselves.

As a former public university president and head of the University of Wisconsin system, currently the president of Syracuse University, Kenneth Shaw knows firsthand the constraints facing leaders on the public side and the challenges before private college presidents. In Chapter Three he makes the case for granting public college leaders the same discretion to succeed or fail that their private school peers enjoy. Drawing on his personal experience at the helm of public and private institutions and research in organizational behavior, Shaw observes that interest groups so constrain decision making on the public side that leaders seek to avoid mistakes rather than to achieve great things. He proposes a reframing of control structures so that public presidents can exercise greater independence in managing their enterprises while still being held accountable for meeting such key indicators as enrollment targets, timely graduation rates, and student learning gains.

Part Two presents two case examples of deregulation in action. Robert Berdahl, author of the classic work on statewide governance, *Statewide Coordination of Higher Education* (1971), studies the experience of St. Mary's College of Maryland, which operates with its own board of trustees independent of the University of Maryland system and enjoys other freedoms from state control as well. Berdahl addresses these questions: Does St. Mary's possess so much procedural autonomy that it has become less accountable to the state than appropriate? Is accountability an end in itself or something to be sought as a means to improved public service? And if the St. Mary's experiment works to serve both the institution's and the public's interest, does it offer valuable lessons for other distinctive public institutions? His study of the success of this one example of quasi privatization leads Berdahl to conclude that the state ought to remain an active partner in substantive questions of mission, goals, and programs. He argues that at the campus level, great latitude in administrative or procedural matters will allow energetic leaders to improve quality, maintain access, and raise more funds privately.

In the second example, Darryl Greer, the executive director of the New Jersey State College Governing Boards Association, describes the ten-year struggle to wrest independence for these colleges from the state's coordinating board. The battle arrayed the coordinating board itself, faculty unions, and the National Association for the Advancement of Colored People on the side of state-wide control against the local college boards and, eventually and decisively, the legislature and the governor on the side of autonomy. In surveying the results of the 1994 legislation, Greer finds that autonomy has led to substantial improvements in the program approval process, in raising money from private sources, and in several administrative areas. Labor negotiations remain state controlled even though the logic of deregulation suggests they should be institutionally based. But the jury is still out, he contends, on the larger questions of the capacity of a presidents' council and other substitutes for the external regulatory power to self-regulate and advocate for collective needs.

The final part of the book focuses on implementing the changes necessary to make greater autonomy work in revitalizing colleges and universities and providing the services the public has a right to expect. Reviewing the various models for state control, Patrick Callan, Kathy Reeves Bracco, and Richard Richardson, Jr., contrast the "indifference-deference" approach that grants substantial autonomy and demands little public oversight with more authoritarian patterns. Based on their review of state-level governance across the country and their analyses on behalf of the California Higher Education Policy Center, these authors conclude that the most effective way of meeting the challenges of increasing enrollment demand, rising expectations for performance, and reduced funding is through a federal model, which permits enough flexibility to enable colleges and universities to adapt to their new and more constrained environment.

Boards of trustees of public colleges and universities must be renewed, Richard Ingram argues in Chapter Seven, if the potential of greater autonomy for these institutions is to be realized. Ingram, the chief executive of the Association of Governing Boards of Colleges and Universities, contends that the membership of the renewed board must be selected based primarily on experience rather than interest group representation or as a political payoff, have the wherewithal to contribute money or know people who will, and be appointed for long enough terms to make a difference in the life of the institution. He lists some exemplary practices in board selection and authority illustrated at Pennsylvania State University, Cornell, the University of Virginia, and other notable institutions. Noting that success of deregulation will rest on the abilities of and the range of freedom granted to the citizen volunteers who govern universities, Ingram offers a useful checklist of the characteristics and the responsibilities of the renewed board.

In the penultimate chapter, Marvin Peterson and Michael McLendon describe and analyze the history of autonomy in Michigan. Peterson, a respected scholar of higher education policy and professor of higher education at the University of Michigan, and McLendon, a former legislative staff member, summarize the contentious history of autonomy in Michigan, then go on to make some thoughtful generalizations based on this chronicle. Recognizing that it can be difficult and dangerous to rely too much on the experience of a single state, these authors nevertheless make several commonsense observations that will help policymakers in considering the shift from more to less regulatory control. For example, the Michigan experience suggests that autonomy will be contested by governors, legislators, and others who wish to control higher education and that informal and voluntary regulatory mechanisms will arise to replace formal control; and enlightened self-interest dictates that institutions be ready not only to compete with one another, but also to join together in coalitions to make the case for resources and continued autonomy.

In the final chapter, I summarize the evidence to argue that relatively greater autonomy can work to strengthen quality and maintain access and diversity, but that the claims that a free market will magically bring greater efficiency and abbreviate costs have yet to be demonstrated. I outline the conditions that seem to be necessary before a state is likely to move to less regulation; suggest specific policies that state leaders, trustees, system heads, and others can pursue in liberalizing control of public higher education; and conclude that we need to retune the relationships among institutions, systems, and the state.

System heads, such as myself, are more likely to argue for greater independence from state regulation than for more institutional autonomy within systems. But as someone who has supervised and worked closely with some thirty university presidents, I have found that greater campus autonomy makes sense chiefly for three reasons. Currently, and for the foreseeable future, the public purse will not match public expectations for more service. Granting presidents greater freedom to use their entrepreneurial talents and creativity is the best way I know to overcome this gap between expectations and resources. Second, too much control breeds a dependent mentality on the campus in which responsibility in matters large and small shifts ever upward. The presidents with whom I have worked performed at higher levels when they held the authority to make their own decisions. Finally, from the modest regional comprehensive to the large land grant with nationally and internationally recognized programs, colleges and universities are one of the glories of our civilization. I am convinced that their ability to contribute to the vitality of our society rests on their freedom to challenge orthodox opinion, pursue truth wherever it may lead, and manage their own affairs to a very large extent. Within this liberal framework, the job of the system head is to make the case for public higher education, to expect much of its leaders, and, to paraphrase Frank Newman, to centralize and decentralize the right things (1987, p. 57).

Acknowledgments

In addition to the contributing authors, I am indebted to colleagues across the country for ideas and critical suggestions. Veterans in the National Association of System Heads, and Bruce Johnstone, its former president, in particular; and the State Higher Education Executive Officers association, especially its able executive James Mingle, have helped me to think through the balance between the legitimate demands for institutional freedom and the need for authority over the collective enterprise. No one should suppose that these colleagues would agree with me on where to strike that balance.

Trustees of the University of Maine system have been as generous with their time in discussing these questions of independence and public responsibility as they have been in carrying out their board duties. The trustees and the very competent presidents with whom I work in this system have been at once thoughtful and courageous in testing out the sharing of power we describe with the motto, "Entrepreneurial universities—efficient system." The senior system staff, notably Mary Ann Haas, Russell Smith, and Sue Huseman, have helped me understand the practical side of trying to implement new system-campus relations, as have Pat Shaw's commonsense insights.

The citizens of Maine regularly debate the value they receive from public institutions. The governor, legislative leaders, active citizens, and opinion makers have hotly questioned whether the state needs more, less, or no university system at all. Many of the ideas presented here were forged in the heat of these public policy discussions.

My wife, Janet Warnert, herself an experienced financial administrator, contributed much to the editing of this book.

Bangor, Maine   TERRENCE J. MACTAGGART
February 1998

The Authors

Terrence J. MacTaggart is the chancellor of the University of Maine system. Previously he served as chancellor of the Minnesota State University system, where he was also a professor of English. MacTaggart has served as a faculty member and administrator at Blackburn College, Webster University, the University of Alaska Fairbanks, and Saint Cloud State University. He served as vice president for academic and administrative affairs for Metropolitan State University, Saint Paul, Minnesota, and as interim vice chancellor for academic affairs for the Minnesota State University system. In 1987, he was named chancellor of the University of Wisconsin–Superior, also holding an appointment as professor of English. Subsequently, he became chancellor of the Minnesota State Universities, serving as the chief executive officer for a system of seven regional universities in Minnesota and a two-year program in Akita, Japan. He is editor of *Restructuring Higher Education: What Works and What Doesn't in Reorganizing Governing Systems* (Jossey-Bass, 1996).

Robert O. Berdahl is professor of higher education and director of the Institute of Research in Higher and Adult Education in the Department of Education Policy, Planning and Administration, College of Education, University of Maryland, College Park. Berdahl has served as assistant and associate professor of political science at San Francisco State College and as professor of higher education at the State University of New York, Buffalo. He was also a senior fellow with the Carnegie Council on Policy Studies in Higher Education at Berkeley. His extensive publications in the field of higher education include *Statewide Coordination of Higher Education*.

Kathy Reeves Bracco is a senior policy analyst at the California Higher Education Policy Center, where she coordinates the center's study

on state governing structures for higher education. Prior to joining the center, she served for three years as a research assistant for
the National Center for Research in Vocational Education, where
she focused on community college and workforce training issues.
She has also worked for the American Association of State Colleges
and Universities.

Patrick M. Callan is executive director of the California Higher Education Policy Center and president of the Higher Education Policy Institute. His prior positions include director of the California
Higher Education Policy Center Study, senior consultant to the
Education Commission of the States, executive director of the California Postsecondary Education Commission, executive director
of the Washington State Council for Postsecondary Education, and
director of the Montana Commission on Postsecondary Education.
He is widely published on the topics of funding, efficiencies, and
meeting rising enrollment demand and has served as a consultant
to educational policymakers.

Rhonda Martin Epper is a research associate with the State Higher
Education Executive Officers (SHEEO), where she served as assistant project director for a three-year project to evaluate and promote state strategies for higher education reform. Her work at
SHEEO has focused on state coordination and governance issues,
as well as statewide planning for information technology, including distance learning, classroom applications, and electronic student services.

Darryl G. Greer is executive director of the New Jersey State College
Governing Boards Association, which seeks to advance the autonomy of New Jersey's nine state colleges. He has been an adviser to
key national organizations promoting higher education, including
the Pew Charitable Trusts and the American Association of State
Colleges and Universities. His extensive publications cover a wide
range of higher education topics: leadership, governance, policy
issues, restructuring, and budget and finance matters.

Richard T. Ingram has been president since 1992 of the Association
of Governing Boards of Universities and Colleges, a national organ-

ization of thirty thousand trustees and chief executives of public and independent higher education. Ingram has consulted widely with boards of trustees and regents in public and private higher education and has written extensively on academic trusteeship. He has edited *Governing Public Colleges and Universities* (1993) and authored *Effective Trusteeship: A Guide for Public College and University Trustees* (1995).

Michael K. McLendon is a doctoral student in the Center for the Study of Higher and Postsecondary Education at the University of Michigan. He has policy and research experience at both the federal and state level, having served as a staff assistant to U.S. Senator David Pryor and as a staff member on the Committee on Higher Education in Florida's House of Representatives. He has authored publications and presented on topics related to his primary research interests in state governance of higher education and federal and state higher education policy issues.

James R. Mingle was appointed the first executive director of the State Higher Education Executive Officers (SHEEO) in 1984. He is the author of numerous books and articles, including *State Policy and Productivity in Higher Education* (1991) and *Goals for Federal/State Policy in the 21st Century* (1995). In 1995, he served as a visiting fellow with Educom, a national organization concerned with the application of information technology to higher education. His most recent work has focused on how states and institutions should respond to emerging technological developments, especially in computing and distance learning.

Marvin W. Peterson is professor of higher education and former director of the Center for the Study of Higher and Post Secondary Education at the University of Michigan. He is past president of several higher education groups, including the Association for the Study of Higher Education, the Association for Institutional Research, and the Society of College and University Planning. He is active in the Higher Education Colloquium, the American Association for Higher Education, the American Education Research Association, and the Council for Advancement and Support of Education. He is the author of numerous articles, chapters, and research reports in organizational and administrative behavior and institutional research and planning in higher education. Most recently, he has written *Planning and Management for a Changing Environment: A Handbook on Redesigning Postsecondary Education* (1997).

Richard C. Richardson, Jr., is professor of educational leadership and policy studies at Arizona State University. His recent studies have examined quality and diversity issues in U.S. higher education and South Africa, statewide coordination and accountability, and quality indicators. He is currently working with the California Higher Education Policy Center on a two-year comparative study of the effects of state structures for the governance of higher education on critical outcomes and with New York University and the Ford Foundation on developing an international dialogue on the future of higher education. He has written numerous journal articles and monographs and is the author or coauthor of several books, including *Fostering Minority Access and Achievement in Higher Education* (1997) and *Achieving Quality and Diversity: Universities in a Multicultural Society* (1991).

Kenneth A. Shaw, a nationally respected administrator and educator, is the chancellor of Syracuse University. He has also served as president of the University of Wisconsin system, chancellor of the Southern Illinois University system, president of Southern Illinois University at Edwardsville, and vice president and dean at Towson State University. Shaw is the recipient of honorary degrees from Purdue University, Illinois State University, Illinois College, and Towson State University and chairs the board of directors of the Council of Independent Colleges and Universities.

For my mother, Genevieve MacTaggart,
who knows the value of independence.

Part One

The Case for Deregulating Public Colleges and Universities

Chapter One

Why the Time Is Ripe for Restructuring

Terrence J. MacTaggart

"Who says organization, says oligarchy," opined Robert Michels in explaining the famous "iron law" that, according to this early twentieth-century thinker, dictates that organizations ineluctably slide toward domination of the many by the few ([1915] 1959, p. 401). The history of governance of public higher education in the United States, especially since the 1960s, confirms this grim prediction.

An enterprise once characterized by relatively independent colleges and universities has become increasingly burdened by a plethora of federal and state agencies and regulations. A few examples illustrate the point. In addition to the Department of Education, colleges and universities must abide by the requirements of the Occupational Safety and Health Administration, the Environmental Protection Agency, and the Internal Revenue Service, to name only three potent agencies, which spew forth a bewildering array of regulations ranging from local zoning and building restrictions to Title IX standards in athletics to freedom of information requirements. On the state level, agencies such as the attorney general's office and departments of employee relations, finance, and administration (again, to name only a few) often not only promulgate rules, but actually manage day-to-day university affairs, negotiating contracts with unionized employees, purchasing supplies and equipment, overseeing construction, and providing legal counsel. Add to this list the host of nongovernmental regulatory bodies like accrediting agencies, athletic associations, and accounting standards boards, and the result is a mind-numbing weight of oversight and constraint.

It is difficult to find fault with the intent of many specific regulations. Who would deny that women should have equal opportunity in athletics or that disabled students should enjoy access to higher education? Yet this weight of cumulative regulation has many negative consequences. In addition to the cost of compliance, excessive regulation distracts the attention of academic leaders from the core educational mission of the academy. A kind of Greshman's Law takes hold in which the need to respond to this agency or that bureaucratic stipulation drives out attention to improving undergraduate education, say, or strengthening research.

The force of bureaucratic regulation and the interests of political leaders in securing responses from the academy also foster oligarchy. The centralization of authority within universities and at multicampus governing and coordinating boards grows in part out of the need to have one point of response to regulatory and political mandates. All of this regulation and centralization, Kerr and Gade point out, "runs counter to the development in American national economic policy toward more competition and autonomy" (1989, p. 117).

Intensifying central authority along with sharply increasing the bureaucracy needed to enforce their judgments, however, is less effective than a relatively more free-market approach to providing the many benefits of public higher education. Management strategies that made sense in times of rapid growth in enrollments, resources, programs, and geographic reach do not answer to the serious challenges facing a mature industry that is adjusting to new fiscal austerity, higher expectations for performance, and the puzzles and opportunities posed by communications technology. Instead there are more effective, less coercive alternatives that suggest that the iron law can be broken to achieve better results.

This chapter examines the pressures that have led to concentration of authority in fewer hands farther from the campus and then notes the beginnings of the countertrend toward greater autonomy. It defines the key economic and managerial concepts employed in the debates over deregulation, presents the arguments in favor of a more laissez-faire relationship between public higher education and the state, and evaluates these claims from a pragmatic viewpoint.

The Iron Law at Work

By the early 1970s, all but three states had established governing boards with consolidated authority over sets of colleges and universities or coordinating boards with some control over at least two governing boards. Aims McGuinness (1994) offers a useful guide to how this massive shift in authority came to pass.

Authority migrated from the campus to the state largely in response to the rapid growth in enrollment, campus size, and programs in the 1960s and the interest of the federal government in ensuring that financial aid monies and other forms of categorical aid were properly administered and applied within the states. If the 1960s represented a period of exhilarating growth for public higher education, state leaders had begun to worry by the beginning of the next decade that too often this growth was unplanned and wasteful. In response, they established various governing and coordinating boards to harness, rationalize, and slow the heady pace of expansion. In addition to this expanded form of control by lay boards, the staff in state bureaucracies and in executive and legislative offices "became more directly involved in both the substance and the procedures of state higher education policy" (McGuinness, 1994, p. 23).

As legislators demanded to know more about and to control the destiny of the higher education systems they funded, the central offices of those systems themselves became more active in regulating campus academic and financial policy. The need to respond to legislative requests for information and expressions of concern over credit transfer or the lack of planning, to cite two common examples, strengthened the hand of central system offices and coordinating boards. The dialectic between the organs of state government on the one hand and system offices on the other meant that increasingly the power to make decisions on what programs to offer and how much to spend on them resided with the system, not the campus.

If legislative interest (some would call it intrusion) strengthened the authority of central boards, the 1972 amendments to the Higher Education Act fortified central power further still. State oversight agencies gathered more formal authority as federal financial aid programs were extended to proprietary schools that required state licensure for eligibility. Special commissions were created at the state level so that federal financial support would be applied within the context of a statewide master plan. Although this requirement was eventually eliminated, nevertheless the federal interest in greater accountability, at least in the eyes of campus leaders, reinforced "state efforts to undermine institutional autonomy" (McGuinness, 1994, p. 24).

During the 1980s the exercise of authority by governing and coordinating boards, governors and legislators (and their staffs), and state agencies focused on accountability for better academic performance in addition to the perennial interest in finances and planning. Thus, a majority of states came to require some form of assessment of student learning gains, and several even instituted incentive- and performance-based funding programs. Inspired by *Involvement in Learning*—the National Institute of Education's call for reform—and other reports (see McGuinness, 1994, p. 24), the quality of undergraduate education, heretofore the province of the faculty, became the territory of national policy organizations such as the Education Commission of the States and the National Governors Association.

State interest in the results of faculty work in the classroom and the laboratory and the chronic concern that public monies be well spent intensified with the nationwide economic distress of the early 1990s. In addition to a pervasive strengthening of the power of existing control instruments, several states dramatically changed the governance structure itself in the late 1980s and the beginning of the 1990s. With a few important exceptions, this restructuring concentrated the reins of authority still more in the hands of boards and state agencies. In Minnesota, Massachusetts, Maryland, Alaska, and North Dakota, legislators and governors restructured higher education with the intention, and often the result, of granting fewer people more authority to meet higher expectations with reduced resources. Governor William Donald Schaefer's desire to "have someone he could call to get things done" in Maryland illustrates the common impulse, although initially the changes in Maryland were not intended to reduce cost (Berdahl and Schmidtlein, 1996, p. 165).

Students of these changes conclude that with the exception of North Dakota, which created a system from a loose collection of institutions, reform through restructuring failed to bring about much positive change. The reasons for this failure are detailed by MacTaggart and Associates (1996). The proximate causes of failure range from lack of political support and inadequate planning, as in Minnesota, to the intrusion of politics and personal political ambition in Massachusetts, to a bungled implementation strategy in Alaska.

Underlying all of these individual reasons lurked a more fundamental problem: a command-and-control approach to bringing about change could not succeed in reining in these complex organizations. The inherent independence of the faculty, buttressed by traditions of tenure, shared governance, and academic freedom on the one hand and the loyalty and self-interest of external constituencies such as alumni, local political factions, and businesses that profit from the institutions on the other, plus the host of other political, economic, and social interest groups that felt they had something to lose or gain in the change combined to frustrate these attempts at highly centralized management.

In addition to idiosyncratic circumstances in each state, there are "perennial" (McGuinness, 1994, p. 19) and often "intractable" (McGuinness, 1996, p. 207) issues that in the minds of governors and legislators demand more centralized authority. Conflicts among institutions and regions of the state, collective bargaining with systemwide unions, unresolved complaints over credit transfer from one public institution to another, and the desire to negotiate a single higher education budget rather than respond to lobbying from several campuses illustrate reasons that policymakers often prefer centralized governing or coordinating structures. The question in most cases is not whether they should exist, but what powers should be reserved to them and which to the colleges and universities.

Commentators like Frank Newman (1987), Clark Kerr and Marion Gade (1989), and Aims McGuinness (1996) have observed that a new relationship, one that recognizes the importance of university self-governance along with the state's interest in accountability and responsiveness to the public's needs, might produce better results. Because of the authoritarian direction of the past thirty years, this new relationship must begin with an about-face in the direction of returning greater responsibility to the academy.

There have been some modest and some dramatic counter-currents to the dominant trend. Illinois eliminated two governing boards but retained its powerful coordinating agency. Higher education leaders in states from California to Oregon to Minnesota and New York have enjoyed limited success in attempting to win back from state bureaucracies some control over administrative and financial decisions. Interestingly, systems themselves, including the California State University system and the University of Maine system, have voluntarily stripped some authority from central offices and returned it to the campuses.

Two of the most striking examples of this devolution of power come in Maryland and New Jersey. In 1988, a major restructuring effort in Maryland bestowed an independent board and significant autonomy on St. Mary's College. In 1994, Governor Christine Todd Whitman of New Jersey eliminated the state's powerful coordinating board in favor of local and relatively autonomous boards for its public four-year colleges. These important cases are the subject of chapters in this book.

Deregulation Defined

Encouraging public enterprises to behave more like private ones and looking to private providers to supply public goods represents the practical extension of American neoconservative thought. It is also a worldwide practice. Developing and mature economies, communist and capitalist governments, and authoritarian and democratic societies actively embrace this approach. So much has been said and written about deregulation or liberalization of private industries as well as government agencies that it comes as little surprise that there is much confusion in the use of terms. One expert in development economics, the branch of science dealing with encouraging growth in fledgling economies, offers ten different definitions in current usage for the term *privatization* (Dhiratayakinant, 1989). This confusion, along with the occasional solecism, accompanied the migration of these concepts to discussions of reducing public control of public higher education. The following lexicon offers some of the widely used, if occasionally inconsistent, definitions of six key ideas: autonomy, deregulation, competition, monopolistic competition, decentralization, and privatization.

Autonomy: Being independent or self-governing.

Autonomy is always relative. Although private colleges and universities and some publicly supported ones have their own governing boards, no institution has absolute autonomy. Even private colleges, such as Hillsdale in Michigan, which eschews federal financial aid and other support, still adheres to state and federal law and a host of regulations.

Deregulation: The removal or suspension of rules or controls.

Removing line-item budget controls imposed by a state budget office, thereby enabling a university to shift funds from one purpose to another, illustrates the term. Robert Berdahl, in Chapter Four in this book, makes a useful distinction between procedural deregulation, which grants more freedom to institutions to make budget decisions, set faculty salaries, and manage construction projects, for example, and substantive deregulation, which could mean shifting the locus of authority over mission and major programs.

Ironically, there are situations in which a shift in substantive autonomy does not include much new procedural autonomy, thereby undercutting the value of the change. Local boards in the State University of New York system, for example, have much to say in the selection of campus presidents—a substantive bit of power—but little control over budgets, tuition charges, or academic program decisions, which remain the province of the system office, various state bureaucracies, or the executive and legislative branches.

In the profit-seeking sector, deregulation of price, locations, and kinds of services offered typically results in increases, often dramatic increases, in competition. Alfred Kahn ([1970] 1995) analyzed the broad deregulation of the telecommunications, airline, trucking, and other industries and discovered greater operating efficiencies and more choices for consumers. But when deregulation makes no difference in the number of providers in the market, their prices, or the services they offer, then it does not stimulate competition and produce the other good things a free market promises. For example, giving public universities the authority to make purchasing decisions up to $100,000 may make for better management but will not affect the supply of and demand for higher education. By contrast, however, should universities actually take advantage of a new authority to change tuition rates substantially, their action could alter the competitive equation.

Competition: A state in which there are options for services and consumers possess the knowledge, resources, and mobility to select among them.

In textbook economics, perfect competition exists when the options are virtually equal—grains or pork bellies, for example—there are plenty of providers, and the market, not the producer, sets the price.

Monopolistic competition: One of the forms of imperfect competition; exists when consumers perceive distinctions among the various goods or services available.

In this case, the prices charged or able to be charged vary with the value buyers place on these distinctions. Higher education illustrates this kind of market in that students (or their parents) are willing to pay substantially more for a baccalaureate degree from an Ivy League institution than they would from a less prestigious state college. Of course, public universities that develop a distinctive image can play this game and charge very high tuition rates, especially for nonresidents.

Proponents of a freer market for public higher education argue that allowing universities to set their own tuition levels permits the market to evaluate the value of their services, encourages those schools to develop reputations for qualitative distinction in order to build revenue, and saves the public treasury some money. Low-income students who would ordinarily be priced out of this market, they say, could be accommodated by siphoning some of the increased tuition revenue into a student aid fund. Those who believe that the market is free enough already point to state and national financial aid programs that act like vouchers in reducing the real cost of private institutions and giving students the freedom to choose among competing options.

Decentralization: A shift in the locus of authority from a higher to a lower level.

Granting a system office authority to seek legal counsel independent of a state attorney general's office or to let bonds for facilities without the approval of a state finance authority, or shifting these and similar powers from the system to a campus, illustrate decentralization in action. Decentralization differs from deregulation in that the rules do not change, but the level at which they are enforced does.

Locating decision making and authority closer to the operational level has become a mantra among management consultants, although some very profitable companies owe their success to highly centralized decision making; McDonald's and Wal-Mart come to mind. Decentralizing often does make sense as a management strategy, but it should not automatically be equated with deregulation or other strategies that increase competition.

Privatization: The substitution of private providers for public ones (Wilson, 1989).

Contracts between government and private firms, vouchers given to citizens so they may choose among private (or private and public) providers, or simply the withdrawal of a government from the market are all ways of accomplishing privatization. Some observers define privatization as any practice that forces public providers to act more like private ones. Judith Eaton, for example, says that "privatizing higher education is not about who delivers, but who pays" (1994, p. 1), in that reduced funding for public colleges and universities forces them to increase their tuition charges, thereby behaving more like their private competitors. Bureaucrats with something to lose by the change sometimes wrongly describe decentralizing authority—to the university level, for example—as privatization. Finally, contracting out or outsourcing specific services—from bookstores to food service to counseling—is a type of privatizing.

The Cases for Greater Autonomy

"The consensus has been shattered," writes Alfred Kahn ([1970] 1995, p. xv) in describing the fracturing of the conventional view that intense government regulation was necessary in public utilities in order to protect consumer interest and prevent the destructive consequences of too much or too little competition. The similar consensus that public higher education needs tight procedural oversight in the interests of preserving access and low cost has been punctured, although the actual process of deregulation has not proceeded very far in comparison with the industries that Kahn describes. This section outlines the basic arguments favoring deregulation along with points of dispute among advocates in the debate.

Universities Are Special

Because their missions are to create and disseminate knowledge, rather than to process welfare claims or issue drivers' licenses, the argument goes, higher education requires greater freedom of action in order to achieve its unique goals. The basic academic freedoms to teach and learn, to conduct research and publish its results, and to express opinions at odds with majority views or the beliefs of powerful interest groups require that higher education be insulated from political, ideological, and bureaucratic intrusion (Newman, 1987).

Of course, to the proponents of tighter control, the very idiosyncratic character of universities creates the need for strict oversight. What else, they ask, will prevent faculty from pursuing increasingly specialized research irrelevant to public needs, administrators from constructing bureaucratic empires, and boards from accepting free tickets to football games but ducking the tough business of saying "no!" to costly new program proposals? In his thoughtful work, *Choosing Quality*, Frank Newman acknowledges that "left totally to its own, the university will evolve toward self-interest rather than public interest" (1987, p. 7). As a consequence, Newman argues, simply granting more autonomy without expectations for improved performance leaves the job half done. A new "relationship between the university and the state" (p. xiii) permitting universities sufficient autonomy to achieve excellence while continuing to deserve public confidence that they are well managed needs to be developed.

Competition Brought About by Deregulation Will Lower Cost

Deregulating business often leads to greater competition, which forces reduced operating costs and lower prices, and often more and better choices, for consumers, at least in theory. The *Economist,* a respected journal of economics and public affairs, reports that regulation alone cost each American household about $7,000 in 1995—more than the average household paid in taxes ("Over-Regulating America," p. 19). In summarizing the effects of deregulation, Kahn notes "substantial price reductions in real terms" (p. xviii) in the airlines and the financial and trucking industries. Interestingly, critics of airline deregulation agree that ticket prices have fallen but assert that "they fell faster before deregulation" (Kuttner, 1997, p. 258). Where costs have not fallen, the additional revenue has enabled managers to invest in improved service and safety. Kahn ([1970] 1995) points to the deregulation of the railroads, where an improved financial status led to investments in maintenance and track repair, which dramatically reduced derailments.

If a chief benefit of greater free-market competition in the private sector has been lower cost to consumers, the institutions themselves and their employees have paid a heavy price. Mergers, acquisitions, bankruptcies, and a continuing series of massive layoffs plague the American economy and society. Arguably these problems are the effects of free trade and international competition, and domestic deregulation has simply enabled U.S. companies to fare better than they could have under close regulation.

The prospect that smaller, less competitive institutions will be swallowed up by larger ones or go out of business, leaving groups, such as low-income students, and communities, such as sparsely populated rural areas, without service causes concern. Should this occur to a great extent, deregulation would have failed the fairness test by leading to an inequitable distribution of this public good of higher education.

In response to these concerns, proponents of greater competition assert that deregulation of business has done a reasonably good job of distributing service. They point to the experience of the airline industry, where small communities by and large enjoyed increases in weekly departures, and many more communities actually gained service than lost it (Kahn, [1970] 1995). In the place of the large carriers that served unprofitable small markets thanks to regulation or subsidy, lower-cost regional airlines have sprung up, connecting small communities with major hubs. If the same holds true in higher education, the students and communities would still be served, though perhaps not by their familiar institutions.

Just as monopolies with their anticompetitive pricing advantages stimulated much government regulation in the first place, so there is the fear that this old shibboleth will rear up again following the current round of deregulation. Combinations of major firms in the entertainment and communications industries, in defense, airlines, and aircraft manufacturing, may represent a return to monopoly or oligopoly. As every student of economics knows, monopoly and oligopoly are modes of imperfect competition that can result in higher prices for consumers and lower operating efficiencies. It is not clear at this point if some new series of interventions will be required, or possible, to prevent a return to the monopoly abuse of the public franchise. A return to monopoly may be of only theoretical concern in higher education, where, in spite of a growing number of mergers among private institutions (Martin and Associates, 1994), it is difficult to imagine any sizable proportion of the three thousand or so institutions consolidating into one or a few entities.

But will the greater efficiency that competition brings to private enterprise spontaneously flourish on the public side? The answer is far from clear. Indeed, there are examples of striking success (Osborne and Gaebler, 1992) as well as empirical studies showing that in perhaps 80 percent of the cases, private provision of public goods is more efficient (Wilson, 1989). Lower labor costs, better management, and the presence of competing alternatives (Wilson, 1989) seem to account for the difference in performance. Yet the success stories are frequently based on instances in which the work processes are well defined and the results easy to measure—fire protection and garbage collection, for example.

In more complex instances, such as K–12 education, the shift from public to private, nonreligious management has shown no dramatic improvement in performance. Efforts of entrepreneurs to manage inner-city schools at a profit have not prospered, although recalcitrant teacher unions and the politicization of school boards are blamed in part for the failure. The well-known experiment with school choice in Milwaukee, where low-income parents have been given vouchers and choice among public and private schools, has yet to produce consistently clear-cut results (Finn, 1997). While not an example of public or private choice, the effort of the New York City schools to decentralize decision making to local boards has led in some instances to fraud, mismanagement, lower student performance, and a plea from one-time advocates of local boards for a return to greater central oversight (Berger, 1996).

The famous exception to this dubious record, of course, are the parochial, often Roman Catholic schools where low-income students from single-parent families consistently perform at higher levels than their peers who attend public institutions. The key variable here is probably not the presence of a free market, which after all does not itself create superior alternatives, but the motivation and support of parents and a tradition of education based on high expectations, substantial time on task, and disciplined behavior.

Better Leadership Will Accompany Greater Autonomy

In writing of presidents generally but particularly those in public settings, a recent Commission on the Academic Presidency laments, "Instead of a leader, the president has gradually become juggler-in-chief, expected to meet an endless stream of individual needs and special demands" (1996, p. 11). The commissioners recommend that presidential leadership, as well as that of the boards of trustees that support them, will be vastly improved with "greater independence from regulation in exchange for demonstrated results" (p. 32). Three former public university chief executives who crossed over to private institutions attest (DeBiaggio, Haaland, and Sample, 1996), as does Kenneth Shaw later in this book (in Chapter Three), to their dramatically increased ability to get things done on their new and relatively more open playing fields. In his remarkable analysis of failed leaders, *Why Leaders Can't Lead,* Warren Bennis (1989) attributes a major cause of the failure to "an entrenched bureaucracy with a commitment to the status quo [that] undermines the unwary leader" (p. xii). In his jeremiad accusing repressive state-level coordinating and governing boards of stifling leadership, James Fisher (1995) extols the courage of Governor Whitman of New Jersey for her willingness to "junk an entire state board" (p. A48).

If leadership in the heroic or individualistic mold flourishes in a world with few bureaucratic constraints, system heads make the case for a collectivist leadership that comes only through coordinated action. Donald Langenberg (1994), chancellor of the University of Maryland system, argues, "By setting common goals, assigning complementary roles to the constituent institutions, and coordinating tactics" (p. 3), system members are more likely to achieve their own and the public's purposes than if they compete with one another. Fisher retorts that "their clumsy, centralized approach to educational planning represents the antithesis of what is needed in today's environment of nimble, customer-focused 'learning' organizations" (p. A48).

What is often missed in the heat of the debate is that the leadership skills that work in private institutions, and at privatized or deregulated public institutions, differ from those in a regulated public setting. Oversimplifying just a little, it seems clear that entrepreneurship, decisiveness, and a willingness to take risks are executive virtues that often spell success (or failure if they result in wrong choices) in private higher education as they do in private enterprise. On the public side, the capacity to collaborate, frame and reframe issues for a broader array of stakeholders, and manage state and system politics are the most important skills. Institutions and systems of universities that shift to a more laissez-faire environment must enable their leaders to develop more entrepreneurial and market-oriented skills or raid the private sector for leaders with these attributes if they are to capture the potential of the new autonomy.

Communications Technology Demands More Nimble and Decentralized Structures

Acknowledging that the full consequences of technology on organizations have yet to be defined, Pat Callan (1994) suggests that models of coordination that relied "quite reasonably" in the past "on economies of scale, centralization, standardization, and process-oriented accountability" (p. 19) will not meet the demands of today's expectations for faster-paced decision making. Others, including James Mingle and Rhonda Martin Epper in this book (Chapter Two), argue that far from encouraging a one-way shift from central to local control, the costs of technology and its complexity require simultaneously central coordination and local implementation. In his apologia for system governance, Donald Langenberg (1994) selects the metaphor of the supercomputer to compare the benefits of integrating circuit chips to integrating institutions for superior results. In the final chapter, I argue that entrepreneurial universities and efficient systems can be had by exploiting communications technology to centralize and lower the costs of many common administrative functions while empowering institutions to use statewide (and nationwide and international) communications networks to extend their reach.

Current Governance, Coordination, and Management Systems Do Not Work

Frustration with the seeming incapacity of public higher education to reduce operating costs, improve productivity, and generate greater responsiveness to consumers finds various targets from the faculty and the tenure system to university leaders individually and, more and more, to its management and governance structures. Fueled in part by the widely perceived failure of higher education as a whole to reform itself (MacTaggart and Associates, 1996), much of the passion for change seems to be fired by an inchoate anger directed at all public enterprises, the national political process, and politicians, corporations and their executives, unions and their leaders, the way the country is run and the direction it seems to be heading. Anyone who listens however briefly to radio talk shows knows the feeling.

Justified by the facts or not, this seething resentment supports change, any change. In his magisterial 1971 study of state systems, Robert Berdahl could judge that "the tensions and disagreements besetting the coordinating process are a lesser evil than either a return to the political jungle, where only the strongest institutions prosper, or a move to direct state administration, which could reduce higher education to mediocrity and uniformity" (p. 270). Today many believe that the third option of deregulation and greater reliance on market competition, even if this includes elements of the economic and political jungle, presents a more attractive alternative to the current gridlock.

Assessing the Claims

Neoconservatives, aptly described by James Q. Wilson as liberals mugged on the way to reality (Gerson, 1996), have been among the most insistent proponents of substituting private for public providers. The ideas of writers like Wilson, Irving Kristol, Richard Neuhaus, and Peter Berger (Gerson, 1996) underpin much of the reinventing government notions espoused by Republicans and Democrats alike. In assessing the several arguments I have presented for deregulating public higher education, it seems only fair to test these claims in the light of the basic principles of their intellectual godparents.

Wilson (1996) contrasts the truly conservative viewpoint that any change is suspect because it runs counter to the "accumulated wisdom of tradition" with more moderate neoconservative skepticism, which holds that "though present circumstances are bad and something ought to be done, it is necessary to do that something cautiously, experimentally, and with a minimum of bureaucratic authority" (p. viii). He contrasts this attitude with the liberal confidence "that if the data reveal a problem, the means can be found to solve it" (p. viii). Good neoconservatives, Wilson would agree, will critically question the supposed benefits of the very policies they espouse, including the value of deregulation and increased competition for public higher education.

How do the various claims for deregulation stand up in the face of a skeptical questioning? I think the argument that the nearly unique (the judiciary and the press, for similar reasons, also belong in this category) features of colleges and universities as creators and disseminators of knowledge and distributors of sometimes unpopular opinion stands as the strongest case for autonomy. To place public higher education squarely under the authority of a governor is as scary in a democracy as arguing that the press should be a creature of the state. Freedom of inquiry and expression are best protected if surrounded by a moat of autonomy, including reasonable independence in administrative or procedural matters.

The argument that a freer environment will attract more able leaders or elicit more creative leadership from those currently in charge is compelling. The testimony and relative success of chief executives who have crossed over from the public to the private side, along with my own experience in tightly controlled systems offering little discretion to leaders and in those which empower their presidents, confirms this view.

Two other claims—that greater competition will inevitably reduce cost and improve service and that technology somehow demands decentralization—are attractive and currently fashionable but have yet to be demonstrated. The migration of students within states and across borders, the unparalleled array of institutions anxious to enroll them, the energetic marketing of public and private colleges and universities, and the entry and rapid expansion of proprietary institutions such as the University of Phoenix suggest that the market is already highly competitive. There is simply no empirical evidence that greater competition will by itself reduce cost, though it may bring other qualitative benefits. As to predictions about the consequences of technological change, James Mingle and Rhonda Martin Epper accurately point out later in this book that we do not yet know enough about the effects of technology to assert unequivocally that its spread favors centralized or decentralized structures. It seems to support both in complex ways we have yet to grasp fully.

Finally, the claim that any change would be an improvement over the status quo clearly overstates the problem. There are overregulated and overbureaucratized systems where the weight of regulation "costs money, stifles creativity and diversity, defeats effective administration and, at its extremes, intrudes upon academic freedom" (Sloan Commission, cited by Newman, 1987, p. 23). States where institutions are buried under multiple layers of oversight from system offices to coordinating boards to state bureaucracies to legislative and executive offices illustrate this level of dysfunction.

In some instances, "mediating structures," to extend this neoconservative concept (Neuhaus and Berger, 1976), be they coordinating or system or local boards, work well. There are striking examples of systems where a sensible structure supports creative and effective leaders (Gade, 1993). In other cases, the crushing weight of the bureaucracy or political interference prevails. The commonsense agenda should be to sustain the former and reform the latter.

This chapter has outlined the major forces that led to increased centralization and regulation in public higher education, appraised the arguments favoring a far less restrictive approach, and suggested that real efforts are under way to fracture the iron law of oligarchy. These themes are treated in more detail and depth in the following chapters. Mingle and Epper, and Shaw argue that the time is ripe for a restructuring of public systems thanks to the push of fiscal and political pressure, the opportunities made available by technology, and the potential for presidential leadership in a free environment. Berdahl and Greer, respectively, describe the dramatic examples of St. Mary's College of Maryland and wholesale restructuring in New Jersey. In the final part of the book, contributors point out how a freer market for higher education can be made to produce better results through changes in state governance policy, reinventing the work of lay trustees, and studying the experience of Michigan, where autonomy reigns. The book concludes with a summary of the lessons that politicians, policymakers, and educational leaders may wish to apply in the effort to free up public higher education for better results.

Chapter Two

Technology, Competition, and Control in Higher Education

James R. Mingle
Rhonda Martin Epper

Information technologies, especially those in the fields of telecommunications and computing, are having a profound effect on virtually every field of endeavor. The convergence of voice, video, and data transmission into integrated high-speed digital networks has spawned a host of innovations in higher education, including a dramatic expansion of distance learning and the use of instructional technology on campuses.

The primary issue addressed in this chapter is the impact of these new technologies on public higher education governance and organizational structures at the campus and system levels. The chapter reviews both traditional and emerging functions, especially those related to instructional delivery, and examines how these functions are being affected by telecommunications and computing technology. Among the educational and planning functions examined are program development and approval, content and faculty development, network development and strategic planning, and student services and academic support. Underlying the discussion of each of these areas is analysis of the centralizing and decentralizing tendencies of technology and the impact of competition and market forces in this environment. The historical traditions of public higher education governance and developments outside higher education provide the context for our discussion. In the final section, we draw conclusions as to the emerging trends in this technology-rich environment and end with some discussion of who will make what decisions in higher education in the future: the consumers (students and employers), the producers (administrators and faculty), or the regulators (governing boards, state and federal agencies).

Technology Developments in Business and Industry

Over the past four decades, American enterprises have witnessed the revolutionary development of information technology, from simple process automation to fundamental restructuring of entire industries. Not coincidentally, this development has spurred rapid growth in competition from around the globe.

The first applications of technology to business operations were in the processing of basic transactions, often where there was labor-intensive paperwork. These early information systems handled orders, billing, accounting, and production control and made significant improvements to company productivity. New technologies also have given rise to better, more efficient manufacturing processes. A classic example is the transforming effect of robotics on the vehicle assembly process in the automotive industry.

In some cases, technology integration has changed the structure of entire industries. Airlines, for example, have become critically dependent on technology for virtually all aspects of their operations. When American Airlines developed the computerized reservation SABRE system (in partnership with IBM) in the 1950s, the airline industry was forever changed. Both United and American Airlines placed computerized reservation terminals in travel agencies, which today generate 70 to 80 percent of ticket sales (Lucas, 1996).

Many businesses have moved well beyond transaction processing to designing or redesigning organizational structures with information technology as a central component. In fact, some business leaders have come to recognize the design of organizations and the design of information technology as the same task (Lucas,

1996, p. 238). Organizational designs in which technology is woven throughout may possess the following characteristics:

Flat and lean. Many businesses substitute technology for layers of management. Decisions are delegated to lower levels of management, placing authority and trust with those responsible for carrying out a particular process. There are no layers of management to look at, edit, and approve work that flows from the level below to the level above. Furthermore, human employees no longer do work that technology can do. Hewlett-Packard, for example, has automated a quarterly wage review of thirteen thousand sales representatives. Software running on a personal computer now does what twenty administrators once did manually (Lucas, 1996).

Strategic alliances with suppliers and customers. Technology enables organizations to establish electronic links with suppliers and customers through electronic data interchange (EDI), electronic mail, and groupware. These links have produced dramatic cost savings by reducing paperwork and facilitating just-in-time delivery. For example, a retailer can communicate with a supplier by allowing that supplier access to its point-of-sale information. When the retailer's inventory dips below an established level, the supplier automatically prepares a new shipment and issues the retailer an acknowledgment of the "virtual" order (Hornback, 1995).

Vertical integration. Rather than forming strategic alliances with partners for mutual benefit, some businesses purchase or merge with a supplier or distributor, a strategy known as *vertical integration.* The decision to integrate vertically is often framed in terms of a make-or-buy decision (Porter, 1980). Should we make our own computer chips or purchase them elsewhere? Should we own our own transportation and delivery service or contract with another carrier such as Federal Express? Benefits of vertical integration include ensured supply and demand, reduction in market transaction costs, and stronger internal control and coordination. Drawbacks are reduced flexibility to change partners and a high capital investment requirement.

Some observers view vertical integration, which can lead to mergers and consolidation, as bad news for consumers. In the communications industry, companies strive to control all aspects of product life, from inception through copyright ownership at the end of the product life cycle (Auletta, 1996). The concern is that mergers of global communications giants—cable companies, Hollywood studios, telephone companies, broadcast networks, and computer companies—will result in too few sources of information and entertainment. Opposing forces equally strong, however, are putting power in the hands of consumers.

The convergence of computing and communications technologies has provided organizations with new opportunities for improved productivity, quality, service, and value to consumers. In most businesses, the adoption of technology has typically come about as a result of pressure from competition, a major financial crisis, a merger or acquisition, a change in top management, or leadership from the board of directors (Lucas and Baroudi, 1994). There have been many casualties in this new technology-rich competitive environment. Companies unable to adapt have been left in the dust, thousands of task-oriented jobs have been eliminated, and thousands of knowledge-oriented jobs have been created. Technology will continue to give companies a much sharper competitive edge in the networked global economy of the future.

Centralizing and Decentralizing Tendencies of Technology

The question of whether information technology induces centralization or decentralization within and among organizations has yet to be resolved. The answer, in fact, may be "either" or "both." One writer on the media, Ken Auletta (1996), argues that the impact of technology on the communications industry has pulled that sector simultaneously in two opposite directions. One pole pulls the industry toward consolidation and megamergers as media companies like ABC and Turner Broadcasting seek mergers with content providers like Disney and Time/Warner. The opposite pole, aided by a political climate fostering deregulation, pulls the industry toward multiple providers (Baby Bells, MCI, Sprint), cross-sector competition (voice, data service from cable companies, and utilities), and individual or small company entrepreneurs (for example, wireless services and Internet providers).

Within large and complex organizations, management must decide whether to centralize or decentralize certain operations. Each option has clear advantages for a company. Centralized decision making allows easier coordination of the activities needed to carry out the company strategy. If managers at all levels are left to make their own decisions, planning can become very difficult, and control can be lost to divergent goals. Centralization also means that decisions will most likely fit with broad organizational objectives. Decentralization, on the other hand, promotes flexibility and responsiveness since lower-level managers are able to make instant decisions. Those closest to the customer are said to be in the best position to adapt to customer needs.

Enter computer technology, and the centralization versus decentralization decision becomes even more complex. Technology thus far has served as a bidirectional force, providing the impetus for pushing decisions both up and down the organizational hierarchy. Information technology has vastly improved the quality and speed of information available to upper management, which can lead organizations to push decision rights upward in the management hierarchy (Gurbaxani and Whang, 1991). For example, bank transactions previously processed locally by tellers are now handled by a centralized data communications system. Also, most nationwide hotel chains are centrally processing customer reservations. At the same time, information technology has helped to improve companies' ability to monitor and measure their performance and that of employees. This has shifted the focus from direct supervisory control of processes to holding lower levels of management and staff accountable for outcomes. Thus, technology can also induce decentralization within large and complex organizations. One insurance company developed a system that allowed it to measure the performance of a salesperson based on the customer's entire portfolio rather that on a per-sale basis. This system increased the scope of decisions made by the sales staff (Gurbaxani and Whang, 1991). In many cases, an organization will choose to centralize some decisions while decentralizing others. Such was the case at Frito-Lay, where drivers and sales staff were provided with handheld computers, which drastically reduced their paperwork requirements and allowed them more time for providing service and building customer relations. The data from these computers also improved senior management's decision-making capacity, thus reducing the need for middle managers who used to gather and summarize data for upper management (Lucas, 1996). Technology in this case pushed decision-making authority both up and down the organizational hierarchy.

Technology Developments in American Higher Education

Like the rest of American enterprise, higher education institutions have been profoundly affected by information technology. Although the changes have not reached as deeply into the fabric of organizational culture as in the private sector, slowly but measurably higher education institutions are witnessing tremendous new teaching and learning opportunities brought about by new technology. According to a recent national survey, nearly 80 percent of institutions have a presence on the World Wide Web, and over half of all public four-year institutions have a strategic plan that describes institutional goals, objectives, or priorities for the use of information technology in instruction and scholarship (Green, 1996). Nevertheless, institutions across the nation are incorporating technology at widely disparate rates, depending in large part on their size, location, and financial resources. While some have made impressive progress, others lag woefully behind in developing basic campus infrastructure and computing resources for students and faculty.

The first and most critical impact of technology in higher education was not on instruction but on administration. Initially, more streamlined and efficient transactions were processed using primarily computer mainframe technology. With the advent of personal computers, faculty also began using word processing, spreadsheets, and statistical software packages.

With the rapid development of computer networks, the Internet, and multimedia software in the 1990s, institutions of higher education have begun to take advantage of technology for improving teaching and learning as well as administrative functions. In the annual survey of campus computing, Kenneth C. Green (1996) reports rising use of information technology in the classroom through a variety of formats. For example, in just two years (1994–1996), the percentage of courses using e-mail rose from 8 percent to 25 percent. The use of commercial courseware in the classroom rose from 11 percent to 18 percent during the same period. Other media that faculty use for instruction include computer simulations, graphics presentations, the Internet, and a variety of video- and audio-based tools to reach remote students.

Providing educational opportunity to students in geographically remote areas has been a major impetus for state-level support of technology in higher education. Since the first PBS telecourses began broadcasting in the mid–1970s, the term *distance education* has been associated with video-based instruction (although its roots lie in decades-old print correspondence courses). Today distance-education media include live formats such as satellite, compressed video, and television courses, as well as asynchronous formats such as videotape and Internet-based courses. Over the past decade, the growth in distance education in the United States has been substantial. In the mid–1980s, only a handful of institutions were offering technology-based distance-education programs, whereas today one would be hard pressed to find an institution (at least in the public sector) that is not at some stage of developing courses to be offered electronically at a distance. Even the term *distance education* seems no longer appropriate given the range of purposes it serves. Not only do students from geographically isolated areas take advantage of this type of learning, but so do students who are balancing full-time work, education, and family responsibilities; high school students opting to get a head start on their college educations; and employers who require programs designed to meet their education and training criteria and need them delivered to the work site (Witherspoon, 1996).

State legislators and governors have recognized the enormous public benefit of extending educational access to as many citizens as possible using technology. Some states have allocated sizable sums of money toward developing a statewide infrastructure and campus capacity to utilize technology more fully. In 1995–1996, for example, New Jersey approved bonds valued at $100 million for technology in higher education; the Ohio legislature allocated $12 million to support information and educational technology initiatives in higher education; and the Colorado legislature approved $20 million to be spent on technology for higher education institutions, K–12 schools, and libraries (Hezel Associates and State

Higher Education Executive Officers, 1997). Governors, especially in the West, also have played an active role in promoting the use of technology in higher education through their promotion and development of the "virtual" Western Governors University.

As higher education makes its way through the "slow revolution" (Gilbert, 1996) brought about through information technology, it faces several daunting challenges. First, support services and training are sorely inadequate at most institutions. Institutions must provide the appropriate quantity, mix, and quality of support services necessary to enable the majority of faculty to make effective use of information technology in their teaching (Gilbert, 1996). Second, providing initial and ongoing funding for a campus infrastructure is a difficult task facing technology-poor and technology-rich institutions alike (Doucette and others, 1996). Resolving this problem will require commitment from both institutional and state leaders to ensure that all institutions have a minimum, basic capacity to use technology. And finally, faculty reward systems must reflect the institutional priority of incorporating technology into instruction. Without this incentive, faculty using technology-based instruction are unlikely to reach a critical mass in traditional institutions of higher learning.

The Choice for Public University Systems: Competition, Regulation, or Collaboration

One of the fundamental characteristics of American higher education is its diversity—in size, organizational structure, and purpose. In the public sector, the majority of institutions are organized into systems under single boards but with dramatically different operational arrangements. These organizational arrangements, whether centralized or decentralized, serve a variety of purposes: to maximize access and/or quality, ensure accountability, gain economies of scale, empower individual faculty, and meet important statewide priorities. For the most part, university system organization is relatively small, and decision making is relatively decentralized. In the words of Karl E. Weick (1976), they are "loosely coupled" organizations.

Overall, this decentralized approach reinforces the values that the academy holds in high regard: autonomy and freedom. At the same time, however, even within a group of organizations arranged under a single board, it creates a competitive environment that can be inwardly, rather than outwardly, focused. This strategy works tolerably well when public systems could be protected from external competition either through state financing policies or regulatory barriers to out-of-state, private, and proprietary competitors.

Public university systems and regulatory coordinating boards have played a strong policy and centrally directed role in moderating internal competition. The primary policy instruments used have been statewide planning, role and mission statements, and geographic service areas that kept the system in a kind of geopolitical balance. These regulatory approaches to program approval and development were also popular among legislators and public officials concerned about "unnecessary duplication."

The use of digital networks, satellites, and cable systems for delivering course work to students wherever they may be has called into doubt whether these traditional "static" approaches to planning and decision making are adequate for a new environment where neither geographic boundaries nor traditional "role and mission" necessarily prevent an institution from launching a distance-learning program. Information technology–based programs, with their different cost structure and economies of scale, also call into question the meaning of "unnecessary duplication" and thus change the perception of acceptability among legislators.

Thus, what we find as a result of new technologies is a state regulatory environment and a modus operandi of multicampus systems in considerable flux. At one end of the continuum are advocates of a completely deregulated system of public higher education; at the other, the maintenance, with some modification, of the regulatory environment to accommodate new modes of delivery. In the middle, we find advocates of a more collaborative model across institutions, not unlike the strategic alliance approaches found in the business sector.

In theory, a competitive model of higher education development and governance would be free of much of the current regulatory environment that controls who offers what courses and programs to whom. More important, a competitive model suggests new funding systems, in the form of student-carried vouchers, that allow individuals to carry their state subsidies to any eligible public, private, or proprietary provider in or out of state. Within this framework, institutions compete on price, quality, and accessibility. Although no state has adopted such an approach, there are a number of trends, unrelated to technology, that point toward this competitive and student-financed model. Rising tuition in the public sector and financing plans that encourage savings or provide tax credits to individuals are but two examples. Such approaches have great appeal to legislators pressed with other demands on state budgets and a citizenry reluctant to raise taxes. Technology and "anytime, anyplace" education may give impetus to this approach.

Although there are obvious advantages to a competitive approach (for example, less bureaucracy and quicker response to emerging needs), there are several disadvantages. Overall public support could be reduced as student-carried subsidies fail to keep up with higher education tuition and other important functions such as research and public service. Moreover, a market-driven system may mean that some kinds of courses that distance-education students need are not offered because they are too costly or because there is insufficient demand (for example, high-cost laboratory programs).

The regulatory approach requires that a central authority, usually the statewide board, reach decisions about which institutions should offer particular programs. Such an approach has several advantages: it minimizes conflict within the system, which tends to result in higher levels of legislative satisfaction and thus higher levels of support; it concentrates public resources on a limited number of high-quality providers in a given area (for example, law, medicine, engineering); and, with its preference for geographic territory, it builds local institutions that become community resources.

The disadvantages of the regulatory approach are especially problematic in a rapidly changing environment. Rather than being a dynamic approach, it is relatively static. Historical roles and missions, tradition, and political clout become the dominant decision factors. A sense of entitlement from traditional providers may constrain state boards from approving new programs in institutions that are more strategically placed and more willing and ready to launch technology-based programs. Moreover, regulatory approaches have often been designed to slow program development, not to accelerate it in response to market factors.

In the middle of our continuum between competition and regulation, we find collaboration, whereby different campuses share common resources as far as possible (such as networks, distance-education expertise, and learning centers), agree out of self-interest to avoid duplication, and collaborate wherever possible on joint course development and delivery. Another form of collaboration is the customer-supplier relationship that develops between a two-year institution with ready and willing students and a four-year institution capable of delivering a baccalaureate course on the community college campus.

Collaborative models have the advantages of synergy among partners with different strengths and increased competitiveness in regard to external competitors to the system. But collaborations, especially in public higher education, appear difficult to negotiate or encourage and take a good deal of time to develop. They often require the catalyst of a central board or leader to overcome initial resistance. Moreover, strong competitors, such as the land-grant university in a state, may see themselves as being held back by the requirement to collaborate with their less well developed partners in regional universities or community colleges.

The Impact of Technology on System-Level and Campus-Level Functions

Technology has an impact on specific system-level and campus-based functions, among them program development and approval, content and faculty development, network development and strategic planning, and student services and academic support.

Program Development and Approval

Information technology has caused many statewide coordinating and governing boards to rethink their regulatory approaches to program development and approval, although no consistent pattern has yet emerged. In an informal survey conducted by the State Higher Education Executive Officers (SHEEO) Academic Officers listserv (Cooper, 1996), most states were aware of the challenges that distance learning and technology brought to their "territorial franchises," but few had made significant changes. (Hawaii and Montana were two exceptions in the West that dropped geographic service areas from their program approval criteria.) Clearly, however, the direction was toward more flexibility and less regulation, either by exempting some programs or tracks from the state approval process or by speeding up the process. In some cases, an implicit "don't ask, don't tell" policy was operating (for example, in the case of Internet-based courses and programs), or informal provisions were developing where approvals were granted for out-of-district programs provided no objections were raised by the home institution.

The enthusiasm for distance learning, which originated with the campuses, has also begun to influence state and system-level decision makers. At least for programs targeted toward working adults, state and system boards have been receptive to program development and expansion, in part because the capital costs of this expansion are found in multipurpose telecommunications networks, not in single-purpose education buildings. A few state boards, most notably those in Indiana and Virginia, have taken a more active role in seeking out new statewide providers of distance learning. With a special appropriation and accelerated review process, Old Dominion University in Virginia launched its Teletechnet program, which offers baccalaureate nursing programs at several community college sites around the state. In Indiana, the coordinating board authorized five public institutions to offer several associate, baccalaureate, and master's programs via telecommunications and assigned those programs specific missions for statewide delivery (Indiana Commission for Higher Education, 1996).

Content and Faculty Development

Given the traditions of faculty autonomy, most systems and campus administrators have played only indirect roles in content development in a technology-based curriculum. At the campus level, overworked academic computer support staffs struggle to keep up with demand from faculty for using Internet-based instructional tools and developing multimedia presentations from existing lecture notes. At the system level, instructional development funds in the form of minigrants to faculty have been used to foster instructional development. For example, between 1994 and 1996, the Oregon State System of Higher Education (OSSHE) provided over $1 million in seed money for institutional demonstration projects in three areas: mastery learning, technology-based instruction, and shorter time to degree completion. Of the thirty-four projects funded, some emphasized interinstitutional collaboration for faculty development and curricular enhancement. Others supported individual faculty members in the redesign of courses using technology. After evaluating these seed money investments, OSSHE is considering more systemwide, large-scale curricular redesign projects rather than continuing to fund (at the state level) discipline-specific innovations (SHEEO, 1996).

The purchase of commercial education software, while growing, remains relatively low on the list of priorities for faculty and campus administrators. For example, in a survey of campus computer center directors in Colorado, four-year research universities rated "use of technology-based commercial curriculum products" as their lowest priority in the overall computing and policy environment for the next two to three years. On the other hand, community colleges and other four-year institutions rated the same item much higher in importance (Colorado Commission on Higher Education, 1996).

This lack of demand may explain why commercial publishers and software companies have been reluctant to make major investments in this arena. Some of the more ambitious efforts have been in the area of remedial math (for example, Academic Systems of Mountain View, California, and Armstrong Labs in San Antonio, Texas) where there is a crossover market with K–12. In at least one state, Oklahoma, the state regents have played an indirect role in promoting instructional software use by negotiating a statewide licensing fee for volume purchases.

In 1996, Educom, a technology-based professional association in higher education, held an invitational seminar for both higher education and commercial interests to explore the market for instructional software (Twigg, 1996). The participants identified a number of opportunities for using instructional software, especially in large-enrollment introductory courses (noting the success of the studio physics and calculus courses developed at Rensselaer Polytechnic Institute), and the necessity of commercial involvement to sustain and update a "scalable body of software" (Twigg, 1996, p. 9) over time. The Educom roundtable also noted some of the constraints against widespread adoption of instructional software in higher education: lack of campus infrastructure, a low priority for teaching in many institutions, and a highly decentralized decision-making structure in academe when it comes to content.

In contrast to many traditional institutions, the University of Phoenix, a corporate institution with over forty-five locations in at least twelve states, has taken a more centralized approach to content development. For course as well as program content, a team of faculty members from around the country collaborate (mostly over the Internet) to create curriculum modules in each program area. Faculty instructors in each location (who are also full-time practitioners) receive heavily annotated lesson plans to follow, resulting in a tightly controlled, standardized curriculum (Baltzer and Slobodzian, 1996).

Faculty development in the use of instructional technology is another area where a voluntary, decentralized approach is the norm. It is also an area of growing priority, as evidenced by the recent survey of campus computing conducted by Kenneth C. Green (1996). The most common forms of support and encouragement provided are release time from class loads and small campus- or system-sponsored training sessions.

One system that has taken a more collective approach has been the Colorado Community College and Occupational Education System (CCCOES). Concentrating its resources on a faculty development and production center on a former military base, the CCCOES is developing a shared production facility with Jones Intercable (the developer of Mind Extension University) and plans week-long summer institutes for community college faculty in the state.

Network Development and Strategic Planning

Many states have seen the necessity for a systemwide approach to developing digital networks for voice, video, and data. In a few cases these statewide networks have been built and transmission costs highly subsidized by state government itself, Iowa being the prime example. Others are partially owned and managed by a state board and system. (For one of the best examples of a statewide "business plan" for network development, see Oklahoma State Regents for Higher Education, 1995.) In other states and regions, network development and management is under reorganized regional networks (for example, NorthWestNet Inc.) following the withdrawal of support by the National Science Foundation and the privatization of the Internet.

Gillespie (1996) notes the following functions of these network operations: (1) Internet connectivity, (2) installation and handling of routers at the campus level, (3) arrangement for leasing communications lines from local telephone services, (4) establishing points of presence that serve rural and low-density areas, (5) help desks and training manuals, (6) representation of state and regional interests, and (7) planning for increased demand and greater bandwidth.

Network management and operations are only one piece of a broader agenda for some state systems. One of the most comprehensive of these initiatives is found in the California State University (CSU) system. The Integrated Technology Strategies project is designed to coordinate system and campus activities in a number of areas, including academic program development, intracampus infrastructure and intercampus networking, administrative applications, libraries and information resources, and user training and support (CSU, 1996). An advisory structure of campus and system-level personnel is built around three major commissions: the Commission on Learning Resources and Instructional Technology, the Commission on Telecommunications Infrastructure, and the Commission on Institutional Management and Information Technology. Underlying the work of these commissions is the overall goal of providing "broad and convenient access to high quality education at an affordable cost" (CSU, 1996, p. 8).

There are a number of advantages for public higher education systems (and all of state government) to act collectively in the development of a statewide infrastructure. Systems gain significant bargaining power and price advantage from telecommunications providers. They can also ensure that underserved areas of the state, which are likely to be neglected by the private market, will receive appropriate investment. From a political perspective, a combination of state agencies, health care institutions, K–12 schools, and colleges and universities have proved to be a powerful lobbying force for significant state investments in infrastructure and network

development. For example, in 1995, Washington State approved
$42 million ($15 million from state-issued bonds and $27 million
from the state general fund) for the K-20 Network project. Through
this enterprise, state leaders expect to improve access to technology resources by interconnecting all users of telecommunications.
Furthermore, an additional $21 million has been approved for
1996–1997 (Hezel Associates and SHEEO, 1997).

The desire for widespread connectivity among campuses and
K–12 has also spawned new cross-sector organizational decision-
making structures. The Utah Education Network is coordinated by
a steering committee with representatives from K–12, state government, and the Utah Board of Regents, the statewide governing
body for all two-year and four-year institutions. This steering committee, with assistance from an elaborate set of task forces and
other committees, sets priorities for system development and legislative requests.

In Minnesota, coordination and development of telecommunications is handled by the cross-sector Telecommunications Council,
created by the legislature in 1993. The council allocates funds and
oversees coordination with campuses, K–12 schools, and six regional
educational telecommunications networks. Prior to 1993, network
development in Minnesota centered on clusters of regional links,
mainly used for sharing resources among schools and colleges by
means of interactive video. Rather than attempt to build a statewide
network that reached every campus individually, state leaders opted
to use the assets already in place within the regions and then con-
nect each region to a statewide network (Epper, 1996).

Network development and strategic planning have clearly had
a centralizing tendency, with leadership initiated at the federal level.
At the campus level, networking and computing developments have
been far more decentralized since the proliferation of the personal
computer. Green (1996) reports that the chief information officer
is no longer the dominant individual in academic computing as in
the past. While this person may take care of servers and networks,
decisions about software purchases, setting up labs, and selection
of personal computers are often made at the departmental level.

Oberlin (1996) notes some of the financial disadvantages to
this decentralized approach. Campus computer support staffs are
being asked to support a variety of hardware with various operat-

ing systems and countless software application programs. This lack of institutional standardization has added significant costs, primarily in support personnel. Out of necessity, the pendulum may now be swinging the other way, with increased control and standardization from the chief information officer.

Student Services and Academic Support

In large part, the improved customer services available in the consumer market have caused today's college students to hold much higher expectations for convenient, technology-based services than those of just a decade ago. Antiquated administrative rituals of waiting in long lines for registration, dropping and adding courses, and financial aid are unacceptable for many students and unheard of for others. In the mid- to late 1980s, campuses began offering touchtone telephone registration, the first of a host of new services that have made life easier for students in the 1990s (Gwinn and Lonabocker, 1996). Colleges and universities, as well as state systems, are looking for the best ways to use information technology to improve service to students and reduce costs. Some of the most recent innovations include consolidated student service centers (for example, the University of Delaware) and placing services such as admission applications, registration, degree audits, and grade reports on a Web site or kiosk for students to use at their convenience (for example, the University of Minnesota and the University of California).

In the area of academic support services, technology is spawning new developments in digital libraries. A selected collection of unique and educationally valuable materials from the Library of Congress and the Vatican Library has been digitized and made available to wider audiences over the Internet (Record, 1996). Some institutions bring academic services directly into the homes of distant learners. The University of Phoenix, for example, offers its on-line students access to full-text databases and other electronic learning resources through its Online Reference and Research Center.

State leaders are counting on these kinds of services to accommodate a growing student population enrolled in electronic-based courses from multiple educational providers. The first visible evidence of the Western Governors University (WGU), for example, will be a virtual catalogue that will contain all course listings, skill prerequisites, and expected competencies for students. The WGU eventually plans to award academic degrees based on accumulated competencies from any number of educational providers (Western Governors Association, 1996). The University of California is pilot-testing a program to allow high school and prospective transfer students to apply for admission electronically to any of the system's eight campuses. Similarly, the South Dakota Board of Regents is developing a single enrollment service center to serve the students of the six public universities and provide support to the campus enrollment management personnel.

Providing administrative and academic services to students electronically can lead to better, faster, more accurate service; reduced complexity; higher satisfaction and retention; and even reduced costs. Cost savings come primarily from reducing the number of transactions that require human intervention and increasing the number of self-help transactions conducted by students. At Babson College, for example, a new student service delivery system set a goal of 90 percent of transactions to be handled electronically by students, 8 percent requiring staff assistance by an administrative generalist, and 2 percent requiring staff assistance by a specialist trained in a specific functional area (Babson College Reengineering Design Team, 1994). Experience in the private sector would suggest that institutions should do their best to respond to student demands for improved services or risk losing "customers" to those with an electronic competitive edge.

Technology Developments in Higher Education Internationally

In contrast to the United States, the development of large, centrally directed distance-learning operations has been the norm in other countries. The Open University in the United Kingdom, founded in 1969, was the first of these mega-universities and has become the model for many, especially in developing countries. Combining broadcast technology with print-based materials and tutorial assistance, these distance-learning operations dwarf traditional colleges and universities in size. John Daniel (1996, p. 31), vice chancellor of the Open University, reports eleven universities worldwide with at least 100,000 students in degree programs. The largest,

Anadolu University in Turkey, enrolls nearly 600,000 students. Similar distance-learning institutions are found in China, India, Indonesia, France, South Africa, and other nations.

Although this correspondence model of instruction is decidedly low tech, the program in the United Kingdom is moving steadily to such technologies as computer conferencing and e-mail applications. Daniel reports that about 10 percent of the 160,000 students enrolled in the Open University use networked computers from their homes, and another 20 percent use computers in their program to some degree (for example, from work or access to nonnetworked software).

With burgeoning enrollments and per-student costs at 40 percent of traditional institutions in Britain, the Open University has long proved its value to many observers in providing affordable access. Surprising to many, however, may be the recent qualitative assessments conducted by the British government. Daniel (1996, pp. 195–196) reports that the institution received "excellent" ratings on six of eleven subject areas reviewed in national assessments conducted in 1995. These high ratings included programs in music, chemistry, and earth sciences, fields not normally associated with distance-learning programs. Another piece of evidence Daniel offers is the frequent use of Open University materials by faculty in traditional institutions (personal interview, 1996).

Much of the qualitative aspect is achieved by a concentration or centralization of curriculum development resources. Course development costs, which run into the millions of dollars, are spread over classes with large enrollments and several years of shelf life. Daniel notes that the quality control provided by central standards and high levels of consistency is especially valuable to countries undergoing rapid expansion of higher education offerings on limited budgets. The "wide distribution and diffusion of responsibility within the contemporary university," Daniel (1996) notes, "makes it difficult for institutions to guarantee quality and coherence" (p. 17).

The Interplay of Technology, Competition, and Organizational Structure

In the complex and rapidly changing mosaic of the higher education landscape, the effects of technology are intermingled with other external forces, especially economic, social, and political forces. We expect, however, that the effect of current and future developments in information technology may be as great as shifts in political climate, tax policy, or demographics. Information technology, with its disregard for political and geographic boundaries, is altering the competitive environment for higher education services, and this in turn is changing organizational structures. The last great paradigm shift in higher education created a relatively ubiquitous organizational model. The current shift in response to the information age is likely to spawn a whole new set of organizational structures and a constantly changing landscape.

One of the dynamics we have observed in this review is the development of centralized service functions in support of decentralized content providers. Both emerging technologies and long-standing traditions in the United States argue against the development of mega-universities along the British model. But economies of scale and competitive factors suggest that institutions will be hard pressed to compete against for-profit or large out-of-state providers without some collective action. More important, student and employer expectations for high-quality programming and services will push public university systems into some centralization of service functions. At Pennsylvania State University, one of the most aggressive distance-learning institutions, the Department of Distance Education was established within the Division of Continuing Education to support distance education across the institution. But content and course development here, and in other university systems such as Wisconsin, remain the responsibility of deans of colleges. In Maine, the board of trustees considered, but then rejected, a separate degree-granting distance-learning institution. The Education Network of Maine is evolving into a service entity providing technical and instructional support to the campuses and direct student services through off-campus centers and sites and through electronic means. We expect shared student services across campuses to grow significantly.

The most significant organizational development in higher education in recent years has been the formation of the Western Governors University. Initiated by a group of western governors but constituted as a nonprofit organization, the WGU has quickly established itself as a new model for the emerging concept of a "virtual university." Its plans are ambitious. Its electronic catalogue will allow students to match their skills, interests, and preferred mode of delivery to a wide range of educational providers both traditional and nontraditional. As an accredited institution it will certify and credential students through compentency-based assessment instruments. As a partner with publishers and other content developers, it will likely enter the lucrative global training and lifelong learning market. Its business plan calls for significant outsourcing of such functions as registration, bookstore, and library support and is likely to include a for-profit subsidiary. That the governors would lend their names, prestige, and energy to such an enterprise is evidence of how dramatically thinking about higher education structures is changing. The WGU has already spawned similar state and system-based initiatives, and its long-term impact may be substantial, not only on higher education structures, but also on the status of traditional credentials and degrees.

A second dynamic we have observed is an increased awareness among public university systems that they are in a highly competitive marketplace for learning. At first glance, it would appear that the public sector is not well positioned to take advantage of an environment that will require entrepreneurial rather than political skills in an education market characterized by volatility and uncertainty. More important, higher education institutions, both public and private, tend to be governed by traditional definitions of quality and traditional (and time-consuming) processes of decision making. They are much more likely, for example, to use technology (like e-mail or computer-mediated instruction) as an add-on to the traditional classroom than a replacement, thus adding costs and lowering competitiveness.

Hemmed in by state regulations on the one side and a traditional faculty on the other, public institutions, critics charge, will be unable to develop new organizational structures and mechanisms to take advantage of a new market environment. For this reason, some observers, most notably Davis and Botkin (1994) in *The Monster Under the Bed,* have suggested that the private, proprietary, and corporate sectors are much more likely to respond to this "learning market" and to use technology in a more cost-effective manner than traditional higher education.

On the other hand, public higher education systems have several advantages on which they can capitalize. They remain the largest and most visible higher education institutions in their states, with widespread name recognition and a residue of public trust and support. Primarily because of state subsidies, their costs to consumers remain affordable. Moreover, their long-standing tradition of extension and public service, especially among land-grant institutions, fits well with this new "anytime, anyplace" mission inspired by information technologies. Public systems also can take advantage of economies of scale when they act collectively, for example, in negotiating for the best possible rates and fees from telecommunications providers or hardware and software vendors. Moreover, proprietary and corporate providers of education and training suffer from their own weaknesses. Although they are more nimble, they have lower name recognition in the education business, higher costs to consumers, and, in the case of the corporate training units, marginal utility to the central mission of the corporation. The last means that it is just as likely that a corporate education and training function will be outsourced to a public university as that it will be conducted internally. (An example of outsourcing to higher education can be found in IBM's operations in the state of Vermont, where the state colleges won the contract to provide IBM's training services.)

It is already apparent that the more aggressive public university systems are restructuring to take advantage of marketplace opportunities. Both the California State University system and the University of Wisconsin system have formed nonprofit entities separate from state controls to market and sell intellectual property. Statewide networks, such as Onenet in Oklahoma, also are leveraging their assets to generate revenue to invest in campus infrastructure.

The third dynamic we have noticed is an increase in collaboration among institutions and across sectors. The growth of the Internet, the lowering of transmission costs, and the growing capability of campus infrastructure to send and receive real-time video have contributed to an extraordinary growth in informal collaboration and exchange among faculty members and institutions. Instructional materials, research findings, pedagogical strategies, and data of all kinds are flowing through a rapidly expanding telecommunications network. The opportunity for faculty and students to collaborate with their colleagues around the globe is virtually limitless.

At the system and institutional levels, this expanded network has spawned a host of new ad hoc commissions, committees, and task forces to solve particular problems: to develop collectively a common user interface for accessing statewide library resources, to launch a new course supplemented by expertise from outside the institution, to conduct a joint research project, to train faculty in a specific software application, to launch collegiate courses in high schools. These informal structures come and go depending on the task.

The constant in this ever-changing web of collaboration is leadership from a system executive, state leader, or institutional president whose job is to stimulate and channel the collaboration. Paradoxically, market forces and the press of competition are stimulating much of this new commitment to joint action. "Collaborate in order to compete" may be the principle around which organizational structures are designed in this new age of technology-based higher education. In a number of examples described in this chapter, we have seen the advantages of collaboration both within higher education and across sectors. These are most notable in the development of statewide and campus networks but are also emerging in the areas of student service and program development.

At the same time, the virtues of a decentralized approach in many areas are apparent. Like business, higher education institutions have an opportunity to become flatter in their organizational structures on the administrative and support side. On the academic side, we expect content and course development to remain essentially an individual faculty responsibility, albeit within a global digital network of resources. But even here, autonomous faculty members will find themselves far more dependent on a team of specialized experts in computing, instructional design, and pedagogy than in the past.

Independence from Whom?

From a public policy perspective, the most important governance questions are as follows:

- How are eligible providers of publicly sponsored higher education programs determined?

- How and in what amounts are public subsidies provided?
- What regulatory controls are in place to prevent fraud and abuse and adherence to state priorities?

From an institutional governance perspective, the most important questions are as follows:

- Who decides what is being taught, what services are provided, and what research is being conducted?
- How free is the institution to conduct its affairs as it sees fit?

Thus, from the institutional and faculty perspective, the primary governance questions relate to autonomy and independence from higher levels of the bureaucracy. At the faculty level of the organization, the evils of administrative oversight from the dean or the president are hardly distinguishable from oversight by a system or state board or "those people in the state capitol."

There is another, and more powerful, governance continuum, however—one that relates to the degree to which the academy and professionals can determine priorities, goals, and content based on their own values versus the degree to which they are driven by external forces. The most powerful of these forces are not bureaucratic structures external to the institution but market forces. Paradoxically, as institutions argue and gain concessions from external bureaucracies (namely, state regulation), they move closer to being dominated by external market forces. Kenneth Ashworth (1996), commissioner of the Texas Higher Education Coordinating Board, in a persuasive essay opposing the Western Governors University, worried not so much about the medium as he did about control of curriculum from outside the academy. Technology is combining with cost pressures to make higher education a much more consumer-dominated rather than producer-dominated industry. In a way, this will make moot the old discussions of what prerogatives are held by the legislature, or the system, or the president, or the faculty. In this new world, the consumers—most powerfully adult students and their employers—may be the dominant governance force.

Chapter Three

Helping Public Institutions Act Like Private Ones

Kenneth A. Shaw

My experience over the past twenty years as a campus president, chancellor, and head of a higher education system in both the public and private arenas has shown me it is far easier to make a difference in a private institution. The ability to make a difference is why chief executives stay longer and tend to be happier than their counterparts in the public sector. DiBiaggio, Haaland, and Sample (1996) note that decision making is faster and easier at private institutions because their presidents have greater freedom to invest in good ideas. They also contend that personnel decisions can be made more quickly and flexibly, and the budget process is considerably more streamlined. In effect, those on the private side find greater authority to go with the responsibility. The biggest difference between the public and private sectors of higher education is that heads of private institutions are free to choose much of the time. They can triumph over problems—and they can make the wrong decisions.

At Syracuse University, for example, we have been confronted with major budgetary challenges, far in excess of anything I experienced in the public sector. In 1991, my first year as chancellor, it was necessary to develop a restructuring and reengineering plan that cut the operating budget more than 20 percent over a four-year period. At the same time, we inaugurated thirty-three major initiatives to move us toward our vision as the top student-centered research university in the United States.

The drastic cut in spending responded to the decline in the high school graduate cohort in our recruitment areas, which was expected to be more than 20 percent over a five- to seven-year period. Our plan called for a commensurate reduction in enrollment rather than trying to recruit more, but less academically qualified, students.

Just as important was cutting budgets strategically in order to help us achieve this vision. Thus, some programs were cut 30 to 40 percent, while stronger areas received budget add-ons, one over a million dollars. Among the initiatives to achieve the vision were plans to reinvent the faculty reward system to give greater weight to teaching, increase the number of opportunities for first-year students to participate in small classes, and increase the number of cross-college minors to help students blend liberal and professional studies. We also provided more than $2 million in funding to stimulate further innovations to ensure that as we became smaller, we became better, especially better at carrying out the teaching and learning process.

The changes made, none of them easy, are working. The proof is in an increased admissions yield, increased retention, increased donations, and increased national recognition, such as the 1996 Theodore Hesburgh Award. Those budget challenges became positive improvements for the university.

This story and countless others that my private sector colleagues could tell illustrate a simple point: it is easier to make things happen in a private institution than in a public institution. The question then becomes, Why not treat public institutions more like private ones? Answering that question requires understanding why and how overregulation in the public sector has evolved. To that understanding, we need to add a program designed to give public institutions and their systems the authority needed to carry out their responsibilities—to give them an opportunity to fail and suffer the consequences, as well as to succeed and prosper.

This chapter traces the reasons that public universities are overregulated and, as a result, unnecessarily wasteful and suggests ways to resolve this dilemma. The resolution includes a change in mindset and gives specific examples of how a new paradigm can free us to think far differently. The chapter then suggests ways to break through the ice of deregulation and begin to create a more accountable environment in spite of an increasingly constrained budgetary situation.

The Problem, or Why Is McDonald's More Efficient and Customer Friendly Than the Massachusetts Department of Motor Vehicles?

Overregulation has strangled public universities' efforts to improve quality, access, and accountability. James Q. Wilson (1989) offers some reasons for this state of affairs. Although his observations relate to federal agencies, they can apply to state governments and their universities as well. Wilson says that a government agency (and many state universities are seen by their state capitals as government agencies, like it or not) dwells in a variety of political environments. Universities and colleges tend to be places where there are many rival interest groups in conflict over goals—a very difficult environment. These agencies, known as interest group agencies, are exceedingly difficult to organize and manage, and often they are sources of bad stress. Wilson contends that these interest group agencies produce both high per capita costs and high per capita benefits. The benefits ensure that constituents will press hard to obtain them; the high costs ensure that the agency cannot meet all the demands equally. Under such conditions, it will always be hard for interest group agencies to know what they are supposed to do since those things that were once rewarded will later be penalized, and vice versa. It depends on which group one is trying to please since not all can be pleased at the same time.

At the external level, among the various interest groups that prey on public institutions of higher education, taxpayers remain somewhat removed from the details of what universities do—except in matters of taxation and access. Then they become highly vocal against tax hikes or raised tuition that could keep their children from attending. On the inside, students will join the lobby to keep tuition low but take the matter of quality for granted.

Legislators and other government representatives form another interest group dedicated to open access while simultaneously making a show of cutting costs. Wilson (1989) says, "The rational course of action for a legislator is to appeal to taxpayers by ostentatiously constraining the budget for buildings, pay raises and managerial benefits, while [at the same time] appealing to program beneficiaries by loudly calling for more money to be spent on health, retirement, or education" (p. 119). And, of course, faculty, a very powerful internal interest group, will press for higher wages and better equipment to ensure that their teaching, research, and service activities are most productive.

Obviously these conflicting interests do not make for easy sledding, nor do they make it easy to arrive at decisions based on the institution's mission. Universities and colleges often end up being more constraint driven than goal driven. Constraint-driven management is pulled to and fro by competing interests and contradictory mandates that tend to be more focused on process and self-protection than on achievement and performance. Virtually every leader I know on the public side confronts this dilemma.

Wilson says the inefficiency of many state agencies (he uses the Massachusetts Department of Motor Vehicles—the DMV—as a base for comparison) in any state, compared with a McDonald's restaurant, illustrates the point. Both McDonald's and service-oriented agencies must serve a large number of people in a short time. But at least in Massachusetts, he observes, getting a Big Mac, fries, and soda in one has been far, far less stressful than renewing a license in the other. To be fair, many users of the Massachusetts DMV report substantial improvements in service since Wilson's critique.

The reason for the poor performance of many public agencies is that they cannot lawfully retain and devote their earnings (or savings) and invest them to improve their services. In addition, many of their goals come from directives elsewhere and thus are sometimes only indirectly related to what actually happens or needs to happen in the agency. Nevertheless, they must be pursued because of interest group pressure. Asks Wilson (1989), "Why scrimp and save if you cannot keep the results of your frugality?" (p. 116). I add, why work hard to improve if, in the end, your efforts will not matter?

One university system I served had its utility budget line broken off from other budget lines. Each of the member institutions was given an annual utility allocation, but any savings accrued during the year had to be returned to the state. In spite of there being no positive motivation for conservation, one enterprising university, with help from the state, made pollution control improvements in one of its power plants by installing specialized equipment. The potential for overall savings was great, but the new equipment created ten thousand tons of fly ash each year that had to be sent to a landfill at an annual cost of $140,000. Through a cooperative effort with another state agency and a private utility company, a process was developed to burn the fly ash in one of the utility company's generating plants—clearly, a potential win-win situation.

The state decided the landfill cost could be charged to the university's utility budget line, with substantial savings accruing to the state, of course. At the same time, the state ruled the university could not use its utility-budgeted dollars for the expense of *transporting* the fly ash. Thus, the university had to dip into its own operating budget, resulting in increased expenditures for its enterprising initiative. The moral was clear to most observers: "Don't expect an institution to find a better way when the culture punishes better results," or stated another way: "In state government, no good deed goes unpunished."

In my view, bureaucracy and the regulations it enforces were set up to deal with pressure groups with conflicting interests. In the process, however, the bureaucracy began to feed on itself, growing larger and less responsive. Nevertheless, its primary purpose is fulfilled: by offering each interest group at least some its demands, legislators improve their chances for reelection. This, in turn, leads to a constraint-driven environment where the worst thing one can ever do is violate a rule.

Obviously I believe in fewer regulations and more autonomy. However, it is important to understand the reasons for the regulation and arrive at creative solutions to help governments out of their own dilemma. Too often higher education's efforts at deregulation speak only to the benefits to the universities and the systems. There will be no meaningful solution if deregulation leaves government with more problems than it had previously.

The Solution: A Market-Based, Accountable System of Higher Education

A market-based system would allow each public university to be both a profit and cost center where accountability measures are agreed to and adhered to. A state government would determine a proper subsidy for each institution. It would probably be based in part on student enrollment, not because that is the perfect way of making allocation decisions but because it seems to be fairly rational. (Any thorough review of the literature on state funding will provide a model for which criteria to use and the weights for each.) This allocation would be a base-level amount, which could be augmented by the university through its tuition charges (specific amounts decided by institutions based on market and other considerations), through private monies raised, and other revenue-enhancing efforts. There would be no restrictions on how the money could be used; savings or profits could be carried over from year to year.

Through mutual agreement, government and higher education would create a set of key indicators to measure each university's performance. At the same time, universities would have their own accountability program to outline programmatic goals, measure performance, evaluate student-learning outcomes, present the results of these evaluations, and describe specific courses of action. Not only would universities improve under this plan, but the effort would also assist government in dealing with its dilemma.

How does this look in action? How might key issues be dealt with in the new system versus the old? Let us look at a couple and then stretch our imaginations a little.

A New Paradigm for Decision Making

New paradigms can alter our thinking about policy issues. Better still, in a less regulated environment, all kinds of new ideas emerge. Many will scare the timid since this kind of thinking is risky. Nevertheless, the rewards are worth the risk.

Issue 1: Serious Compensation Problems

Let us say the faculty are underpaid compared with their market contemporaries. (If the market is defined as the midpoint in a range made up of peers, half of the institutions will fall below the mark.) Under the old model, the university lobbies state government for a solution. The case is made again and again, pressure is applied, and perhaps something is done if there is funding available; usually there is not.

Under the new model, the university is given a set amount, told it can raise revenue through tuition and other sources, and is permitted to free up money through staff and faculty reductions and operating budget reallocations. In other words, it has its state allocation and the tools to deal with its particular salary situation in the most effective way it can.

There are trade-offs, of course. More money for salaries means increasing the amount of money available by raising income through tuition, decreasing the number of people in salaried positions, decreasing operating funds, or any combination of the three. In other words, the state in effect says, "Don't waste time with impressive facts and figures. If you need to pay faculty more, use the money allocated to you and the flexibility we've granted you."

Issue 2: Faculty Teaching Load

This is a familiar refrain. The state commissions a study that shows faculty "work" only nine hours a week, and if they would just put in another three hours of "work," a lot of money could be saved. The institution or system counters with another study showing that faculty spend more than fifty-five hours a week teaching, advising, preparing, and doing their scholarly work. After considerable posturing, usually very little is accomplished; the only results are a great waste of time and an annoyed public.

Under the new model, if the faculty load is really too low, the university must raise tuition since the state subsidy will not meet instructional requirements. Too high a tuition, though, will diminish enrollment. The hard decisions are left in the university's hands, and it is charged with meeting the need. This, in my view, is preferable to the current generation of unproductive heat and noise between the state and the university but very little concrete change.

Issue 3: New Buildings

Under the old model, when new construction or renovations are needed, the university makes a strong case and enjoins area legislators, union leaders, and others to rally to the cause. Buildings, after all, are gratifying projects, made doubly so since the state pays for them. Because that is the case, universities have little reason to weigh the pros and cons of new construction fully. In response, the state develops a bureaucracy to deal with the manifold requests while the universities work at outmaneuvering each other for a bigger piece of the building pie.

Under the new model, funds would be built into the annual budget to be used for new buildings and renovation as part of the upfront allocations. Institutions could decide to spend no money on construction (and in a short time have a crumbling infrastructure, a much lower enrollment, and a deposed president) or strategically plan for expenditures for this purpose. Since money could be carried over, they might save for a major project or use a portion of the operating budget to bond a major initiative or several initiatives. Government would not be pressured by various interest groups that want new buildings. Universities would not waste time and money lobbying, instead reserving their energies and funds for the proper growth and maintenance of their physical plants and for carrying out their primary missions.

Issue 4: Privatization

Suppose a state decided it needed to get more for its dollar in higher education. Knowing the next demographic bulge will require far more money than will be available, this state looks past traditional boundaries. It might decide to include independent institutions as part of the mix, since in many situations it could be cheaper to subsidize private higher education at a low level than it would to expand in the public arena.

Issue 5: What to Do with the Crown Jewel?

Every state has a public institution that is seen as the crown jewel—usually the land-grant institution. Since it can afford to be very selective in admissions, it might find it can raise tuition there quite a bit and still be market competitive. I contend that most "jewels" could raise tuition to probably 75 percent above the average tuition of public institutions in the state and hold a strong market position. Access could be maintained by setting aside perhaps as much as 25 percent of this new money for financial aid. This is what private institutions have been doing for a long time. Like their private counterparts, the state jewels would let the market determine what they could charge and how much they would put back into financial aid. The primary benefits would be a greater responsiveness to students and greater financial resources for quality and growth.

More Accountability with Less Regulation

How do we hold institutions accountable when we have taken away most of the controls? Here, key indicators could be developed to measure performance. Policymakers could use that information to help determine how much subsidy an institution might receive. These key indicators could include such factors as quality of instruction, graduation rate, retention rate, diversity, yield rate of admission offers, and overall financial performance. Also, each institution would be expected to have not only a well-defined institutional mission statement but mission and goal statements for each programmatic areas. Each institution and program would be required to outline its plan for evaluating student learning outcomes and presenting those findings each year plus changes in teaching methods, curriculum, and so on necessary to improve outcomes. Performance audits could also be used more frequently and more effectively.

There would still be controversy—over the size of the subsidy for higher education, over the appropriateness of the assessment criteria used, and over whether goals were reached. But at least the new process would focus on important issues affecting education. It would also allow the universities the authority that should accompany responsibility.

How State Government and the Universities Might React

So far, no one seems to be interested in such a plan. States that have deregulated have done so on the margin, and the mind-set is still that of a constraining environment rather than a goal-oriented environment. (Perhaps the universities of Michigan and Pennsylvania are notable exceptions.) Universities continue to seek less regulation but offer little to demonstrate their commitment to increased accountability for educational performance.

A proper development plan might appeal to state government for two reasons. First, universities would be better managed and more cost-effective. Fewer funds would go to supporting the bureaucratic bloat now necessary to deal with the various rules and regulations. More time at the state, system, and campus levels could be spent on substance. Dollars would be allocated based on mission and goals and priorities set at the institutional level. Second, special interest pressures would focus where they belong: at the college and university level. Once funding limits were set and a set of indicators and assessment policies and practices put in place, state governments' primary responsibilities would be met. All other issues would be sent to the institutions to resolve. Along with the freedom comes the heat, and Harry Truman reminded us what people can do about that if it gets too hot in the kitchen.

The government, of course, will present objections to these changes. First, they are alien, different from the way things have always been done. Second, they might be seen as a loss of control. That is true, of course. But in this world competitive market, change is the order of the day. Major corporations have had to decentralize radically or disappear. If state officials want colleges and universities to prosper, now is the time to introduce greater flexibility and entrepreneurship.

The universities would applaud some of the new autonomy. I know they would like the greater flexibility and the greater authority. The far greater responsibility might be less palatable. Success and failure could be more easily pinpointed, and not all would like that. Goals are difficult to develop and measure. Things might really change. Probably fewer buildings would be built under this model. Campuses would need to be more entrepreneurial and adept at fundraising or go under. And the institutions themselves would have more internal controversy because they could not blame government or the system office for their problems. For some, the suffocating blanket of overregulation at least allows a slow death where bad performance in a competitive market would be fatal more quickly.

The Next Step

This break through the ice of deregulation begins with a change of attitude. State governments and higher education can begin by acknowledging that some regulations have served the citizenry well, while others have led to a constraint-based mode of operation that is costly and far from being results oriented. Second, both entities could engage in a dialogue about specific performance indicators. By coming together, government and higher education could develop meaningful sets of measurements, which could be reviewed and revised as necessary.

Third, higher education could engage in dialogue with government regarding the proper role of assessment. Virginia and Illinois and a few other states have pursued such discussions. Finally, discussions could begin about a set of protocols to make such a system work. These protocols must be attentive to the needs of the institutions to serve their missions in the most efficient and effective way; further, they must be attentive to the needs of government to keep it free from undue pressure from special interests.

Conclusion

Regulations were developed and continue to exist to ensure the public benefits and to deal with those competing pressures and issues peculiar to high-cost, high-benefit agencies. That they have become constraint driven and for the most part dysfunctional should surprise no student of organizations. If institutions of higher education want to achieve greater flexibility, they must understand why these structures were set into place and provide ways for government to protect its interests.

True flexibility will come at a price. That price might be mutually agreed-on specific indicators, agreed-on mission and goal statements for institutions and programs, and an effective way to evaluate outcomes. What is needed now is a state and a system of higher education with the imagination to deregulate radically for better performance.

Case Examples of Deregulation in Action

Part Two

Case Examples
of Deregulation
in Action

Chapter Four

Balancing Self-Interest and Accountability: St. Mary's College of Maryland

Robert O. Berdahl

Recent favorable changes in the national economy have been reflected in improved fiscal conditions in many states, making it less likely that public universities and colleges will face immediate stringent pressures for budgetary cutbacks. But another wave of enrollment increases in the next ten years suggests one can anticipate continuing state pressures for cost containment. A few years back, public policy choices were to "do more with less," failing which one could do "less with less," reducing access, or "do less well with less," reducing quality. With better fiscal conditions and higher enrollment projections, one might now hear "do more with not much more"! St. Mary's College is a case study of this effort.

This chapter takes up one of the possible policy choices involved in trying to do more with less: giving a state institution a hybrid public-private status by state law, to see whether privatizing some of its functions would allow it to become so efficient and effective that it could increase quality, maintain access, and raise increasing amounts of funds from nonstate sources. In other words, the state would not appropriate more tax dollars to support the institution; rather, it would give the institution more procedural autonomy (flexibility) to spend the dollars it does receive.

The case study concerns the 1992 Maryland legislation that granted St. Mary's College, a public honors college, a lump-sum budget and exemption from most state controls (for example, over procurement, personnel, and some capital development processes) in exchange for an institutional agreement to cap state tax support at a mutually agreed level (plus future growth to cover inflation). In addition, St. Mary's College agreed to use some of the additional tuition income from the institution's plan to double its tuition charges in five years (from $2,500 to $5,000) to maintain the access of low-income students.

The policy question emerging from this set of facts relates to whether the changes turn out over time to be win-win for both the institution and the broader public interest or whether informed opinion at the campus or in the state capitol perceives the changed status not to have been in the best interest of either the institution or the state or both. Admittedly, the term *public interest* is subject to varying interpretations, but this analysis uses the notions of the tensions between autonomy and accountability advanced in the opening chapter of my book, *Statewide Coordination of Higher Education* (1971). According to this analysis, one first distinguishes between an institution's claim to academic freedom and its hope for maximum autonomy. Academic freedom is defined as the freedom of the individual scholar in his or her teaching and research to follow truth wherever it seems to lead without fear of punishment for having offended some political, religious, or social orthodoxy. This freedom is considered so fundamental that legitimate governmental action abridging it is nearly unthinkable.

In contrast, all public sector institutions operate in a legal and political environment in which autonomy issues have to be played out in the context of the institutions' general accountability to the public interest, as interpreted by actions of the current executive and legislative branches. Here it is helpful to distinguish between notions of procedural autonomy and those of substantive autonomy. The former are essentially matters of means—the how of academe, that is, the processes by which institutions pursue their substantive goals. The latter are the actual goals, purposes, and functions that constitute the core reasons for existence of the institutions in question—the what of academe. By this analysis, state accountability patterns that affect procedural autonomy may sometimes seem irritating or even counterproductive to the institutions, but they usually do not prevent the ultimate achievement of institutional goals. In contrast, state accountability patterns that affect substantive autonomy raise crucial questions about which kinds of decisions need to be made at which locations for the autonomy-accountability tensions to be worked out in ways that allow both the institutional needs and the public interest to be well served.

Applied to this case study, the operating questions become: Has the state granted so much procedural autonomy to St. Mary's College that the necessary ingredients of accountability have been lost? Is accountability an end in itself, or a means toward the efficient and effective delivery of public services? If the case of St. Mary's College seems to indicate that both sides have gained from the agreement, are there precedents involved that could be extended more broadly to the public sector of higher education?

With an event this recent, an investigator has no choice but to supplement the meager written record with extensive interviews of key actors at both the campus in question and among persons in the state capitol and elsewhere who were involved or have had relevant opinions on the desirability of the changed status. In order to encourage maximum candor, I promised respondents confidentiality. I interviewed twenty-three persons: twelve associated with the campus and eleven scattered across the executive and legislative branches of state government, the state coordinating board, and other public sector institutions. In situations where nuanced judgments are crucial, survey data do not serve the purpose. Face-to-face interviews, with the opportunity to inspire respondent confidence in the investigator's ability to come well prepared and to be discreet in the use of sensitive information gained, provide much richer data.

Events Leading to the 1992 Law

Most higher education institutions with good public relations offices issue pronouncements about the "uniqueness" of the particular institution's evolution. In the case of St. Mary's College of Maryland, there truly are unique circumstances surrounding its origin and evolution. It started life in 1840 as a public secondary boarding school for women, St. Mary's Female Seminary. It was created by state law as a living monument to the memory of the state founders, who, on

that very site in 1634, had established the state capital, which was to
last until 1694 when the capital was moved to Annapolis. From 1840
to 1923, the seminary struggled to survive the vicissitudes of civil war
and modest enrollments. In 1923 the seminary added the words
"Junior College" to its title and expanded to a six-year curriculum.
In 1935 it was decided to drop the first two years of secondary
schooling and the institution became a four-year junior college.

World War II brought some growth to the rural area in which
the college was located (including some national military facilities),
and some men were allowed to study there, either as nonresidential
day students or evening students. In 1947 a state commission on
higher education, the Marbury Commission, recommended a statewide system of locally controlled junior colleges but urged that several public institutions, including St. Mary's, be closed—in the case
of St. Mary's, because its relatively high cost per student and its rural
location seemed to preclude its becoming minimally efficient. The
college was able to block that recommendation and in 1960 gradu-
ated its last class of high school seniors, becoming for the next eight
years a coeducational junior college. But a Middle States accrediting report was critical of what was perceived as unresolved tensions
between the traditionally oriented liberal arts day programs and the
more vocationally oriented evening programs. Deciding to concentrate on its historic emphasis on the liberal arts and ignoring a
Middle States warning about moving too quickly toward four-year
college status, the institution in 1964 applied for and received state
approval to become a public four-year liberal arts institution, named
St. Mary's College of Maryland. The long transition from secondary
seminary for women to liberal arts college for all was completed.
(For more details of the fascinating history, see Fausz, 1990.)

The college created a new general studies curriculum in 1985
and continued its steady climb in the number of applications received and in the average Scholastic Aptitude Test (SAT) scores of
entering freshmen. Perhaps more important, the college under the
leadership of Edward (Ted) Lewis carefully built an increasingly
prestigious board of trustees and recruited a powerful group of experienced senior administrators.

When Governor William Donald Schaefer proposed a massive
reorganization of public higher education in Maryland in 1987,
St. Mary's College resisted the move to consolidate the governance

of all public four-year institutions under one governing board. This proposal was spearheaded by John Toll, president of the University of Maryland system, and was endorsed by the heads of all other but one of the state's public four-year colleges. The other resisting institution was Morgan State University, a predominantly black institution in Baltimore. The power of the legislative black caucus in the state legislature was sufficient to exclude Morgan State from the later merger, and it must have been the power and political prestige of St. Mary's board of trustees that also permitted them to resist the strong pressures from the executive and legislative branches for total merger.

The configuration that resulted (Berdahl and Schmidtlein, 1996) in 1988 encompassed a merged University of Maryland system (with five former university campuses and six former state college campuses); a separate St. Mary's College with its own board of trustees; a separate Morgan State with its own governing board; a system of seventeen community colleges, each with its own governing board; and a large private sector. All were presided over by a revamped state coordinating board, the Maryland Higher Education Commission, which had replaced a weaker State Board of Higher Education.

The good news for higher education in the state was that the governor had promised to increase significantly state funds going to higher education if the institutions agreed to substantial reorganization, and he evidently believed that the changes accomplished sufficiently met that goal, for state appropriations to higher education increased from $614 million in fiscal year (FY) 1988, to $700 million in FY 1989, and $821 million in FY 1990. Those are large increases by any measure, and all institutions, including both Morgan State and St. Mary's, welcomed strong budget support. St. Mary's appropriations increased from $6.8 million in FY 1988 to $7.8 million in FY 1989 and $8.9 million in FY 1990.

To the increased state funds going to St. Mary's were added those coming from an increase in annual giving (from $30,000 in 1983 to $335,000 in 1992) and those resulting from the five-year Campaign for National Prominence, instituted in 1989, which raised $16.3 million by the end of 1992: $5 million over goal and two years early. This campaign aimed to raise funds not only to improve academic and physical plant resources but also to enlarge the faculty, thereby reducing the student-faculty ratio. This ratio had declined from 16:1 in the late 1980s to 13.6:1 in 1994, with long-range plans calling for a 12:1 ratio.

The bad news with respect to state support was that, as happened in many other states, the bottom dropped out of the Maryland state economy in 1991–1992, and state support for higher education nose-dived from $821 million in 1990 to $715 million in 1992. However, in contrast to stand-still or slightly cut budgets for most other public institutions (some predominantly black institutions received small increases), St. Mary's College was granted another substantial increase in 1991, to $10.4 million, before suffering a series of 1992 cuts, ultimately receiving $9.2 million, or an estimated reduction of about 12 percent of total budget. Clearly the institution and its trustee luminaries (the board included Andrew Goodpaster and Paul Nitze from national security sources; Ben Bradlee from the *Washington Post;* Steven Muller, president emeritus of Johns Hopkins University; and Ben Cardin, former Speaker of the Maryland House of Delegates and then congressman in the U.S. House of Representatives) had been able to convince the Higher Education Commission and the state executive and legislative branches that it was a special college, accomplishing special work, and therefore deserving of increased state support even in difficult times. But just as obviously, there were limits, and the state had seemed to reach them.

It was at about this time that some crucial judgments were made and some high-risk decisions taken. It was the best estimate from President Lewis and the high-powered board that the state's severe fiscal crisis was not going to be just a momentary condition, to be ridden out until better times came along. Instead, the leadership looked at the growing national debt, the annual national budget deficits, the need to anticipate politically explosive cutbacks in social security and medical programs, the probable efforts to transfer to state responsibilities certain functions and funding currently provided by the federal government, and, not incidentally, the particularly devastating impact on the Maryland economy because of the state's strong links to so many federal offices and military bases scheduled for retrenchment. They judged that the institution should not go into a holding pattern awaiting a better day; rather it should exploit a series of strong cards it held to seek a special relationship with state authority and state funding.

The Transition to Hybrid Public-Private Status

In 1991, in the midst of the state fiscal crisis, Governor Schaefer issued a challenge to the colleges and universities. In the words of Shaila Aery, the secretary of higher education and chief executive officer of the Maryland Higher Education Commission, this challenge was "to explore creative new strategies for financing higher education. The state budget already had suffered severe cuts, and deficits were predicted through the end of the decade. It had become obvious that status-quo funding for higher education for the remainder of the decade was the new economic reality. Those of us in the higher education community knew fundamental changes were in store for our colleges and universities and their relation to the state" (Lewis, 1994). Following up on the governor's statement, Aery then outlined a range of options, one of which was that institutions be granted "increased flexibility and authority in management, personnel and budgetary decisions, enabling them to be more efficient and productive while containing costs" (Lewis, 1994).

St. Mary's College was in a unique position to exploit this alternative for a variety of reasons. It had established a firm market niche as a low-cost public sector equivalent to some of the finer private liberal arts colleges (for example, Davidson, Franklin and Marshall, Colby, Hamilton, and Bates), so it could raise tuition charges substantially without threatening its needed enrollments. It had a strong track record for already having made itself into an institution of considerable diversity and could therefore presumably be trusted not to let its higher tuition charges turn it into an upper-middle-class preserve. It had a strong board of trustees that could reassure the state that prudent use would be made of any newly granted freedoms and could also continue the excellent fundraising already evidenced in the Campaign for National Prominence. Finally, it had a leadership team that accepted the risks posed by a determination to make the new relationship work.

What were these risks? As the careful negotiations pursuant to the passage of House Bill 1327 occurred in 1991–1992, three sets of trade-offs were involved. First, in exchange for receiving a lump-sum appropriation and procedural autonomy regarding personnel, procurement, and capital development projects funded with nonstate funds, the institution agreed to cap its operating budget request to the state to the amount appropriated in 1993 (back up to $10.38 million), inflated in future years only as indicated by the implicit price deflator for state and local government [House Bill 1327, sec. 14–205, B 1,2 (I)(II)]. Clearly the risk here is that the state economy might quickly recover, and the other noncapped public institutions (and those private institutions receiving state funds with an escalator clause tied to 16 percent of the funds appropriated public four-year institutions) would receive increases in state funding far larger than that generated by the implicit price deflator. If such were to occur, the newly granted procedural freedoms might seem to have been purchased at too high a price.

Of course, logically, the opposite scenario must also be considered. If the state's fiscal problems were to become much worse, rather than status quo or better, then the cap would act as a floor, and the state guaranty would protect St. Mary's tax appropriations in a way that would not legally apply to the other institutions. To be sure, protective language in the bill (and in the later memorandum of understanding between the governor and the college) says that the "predictable level of funding" does not in any way "restrict the budgetary power of the General Assembly" [14–205, B (4)]. So in cases of a "fiscal crisis of large and pressing proportions," according to the memorandum, the state would be able to reduce the promised appropriations to St. Mary's. But, in theory, if the state's fiscal crisis were of a lesser nature, the state would continue to provide the same predictable level of funding plus that generated by inflation.

Second, although the institution already had the power to set its own tuition charges, politically it would have been unacceptable to double them (from $2,500 to $5,000) in five years without having promised to use some of the additional income as institutional student aid to affirm "the need for increased access for economically disadvantaged and minority students" [sec. 14–204, E (iv)]. Here the risks are that the projected student demand might not be sufficiently strong to meet the future budget growths predicated on increased tuition income and that broadened student access might not be achieved, even with a larger proportion of institutional funds going into student aid.

Finally, receiving lump-sum state appropriations and immunity from state personnel and procurement controls would allow the institution to undertake academic innovations and quality enhancement projects of its own choosing, but such innovations and projects could not be achieved unless the capped state appropriations and larger tuition income could be supplemented significantly through enlarged private giving. The increased tuition income would have to be reduced by sizable amounts diverted to increased student aid funds. Thus, for increases in faculty numbers and faculty salaries, new academic programs, or improved library or student services, for example, the institution would have to rely more on private giving and less on state tax dollars. A projection of estimated income showed the state share of the St. Mary's total budget declining from about 50 percent in 1992 to 40 percent in 1997, with further decline anticipated after that. The obvious risk was that the increase in private giving might not be sustained over time, and the amount of new money for innovations and quality enhancement might be less than projected. One advantage of the cap-floor was that presumably the state appropriations would not be reduced even if the private fundraising were to be very successful.

Once the senior leadership at St. Mary's was convinced that the potential benefits of a new relationship with the state were worth the various risks, a careful campaign was undertaken to get each of the college's constituencies to buy in on the process. The board of trustees was involved from the start. Ed Clarke, the former chair, used his considerable legal skills to help draft the legislation in a way that would establish the new relationship in a manner mutually acceptable to the institution and the state. The current chair, Steven Muller, president emeritus of Johns Hopkins University, was able to ensure doubting trustees that the proposed changes were in fact "a pragmatic, effective response to a changed environment" (Lewis, 1994). Then, President Lewis later reported, "Thorny discussions continued [at board meetings]. The trustees asked us to revise our cash-flow analysis—inflating expenditures by 4 percent to 5 percent and cutting projected revenues from the private sector. They cautioned us to factor in escalating health care costs. They grilled us about how the union would react to the college's declassification of its support staff. Senior administrators were pushed and even, at times, appropriately bullied. And when the proposed bill went before the legislature for discussion and vote, we were ready" (Lewis, 1994).

The St. Mary's faculty were not hard to persuade of the merits of the change. Already plans included both expanding the number of faculty and increasing their salaries. Furthermore, the very act of having been designated in 1991 as a public honors college had had something of a Hawthorne effect; it seemed more prestigious to be teaching at a place singled out for such a special designation. A public honors college is a liberal arts college in the public sector whose entire student body will take what is widely considered to be an honors-level curriculum.

A college task force on the new status was created, with some membership drawn from the campus senate. Later a secret ballot was taken among faculty ranks; if my respondent was understood correctly, only one abstention was reported.

A little later, in 1993, the college restored tenure, which it had taken away in 1971 and replaced by a contract system. This restoration was done in order to give faculty a stronger motivation to identify their professional futures with the institution and, not incidentally, to provide for a more rigorous formal tenure evaluation process.

Staff had to negotiate their legal status if they gave up the protection of being members of the state civil service. They were given until July 1, 1993, to decide whether to transfer to the personnel system established by the college, with those declining the transfer to receive "job counseling and placement services for either a State or private sector position" (11–203, sec. 2). Presumably they were giving up being covered by future state cost-of-living adjustments (COLAs) but would be receiving instead college merit increases based on performance evaluations. Only one employee declined to transfer to the new system.

Alumni as well were kept informed of developments, with differential reactions reported depending on how far back their college experiences had occurred. Those associated with the college before the 1980s seemed somewhat less concerned than more recent graduates, who evidently sensed that their own records could only be enhanced by the improving image and reputation of their alma mater.

Students and their parents were not ignored. A letter from President Lewis to "Students and Families" on November 25, 1991, laid out the case for the changed status of the college. The various cuts in state appropriations during the preceding year were outlined and mention made of the dangers if further cuts were necessary. The letter speculated that after initial reductions already made in budgets for continuing education, public safety, and health services, the college might have to phase out some academic majors and reduce the overall number of courses, "making it more difficult for students to complete their degrees in the normal four years." The plan to raise tuition from $2,500 to $5,000 over the next five years was introduced, with the explanation that some of the additional income would be used to expand student aid: "No student admitted to the College would be forced to drop out because of a clear financial need." Families were urged to discuss the letter over the Thanksgiving break, and then students would have an open forum on December 2 to bring up their concerns. The process evidently went smoothly; students and families seemed to buy in as well.

With all of these careful preparations, the stage was set for a smooth legal transition. Since both the governor and the secretary of the Higher Education Commission were strong supporters, most executive branch senior staffers swallowed whatever misgivings they might have had about either or both of the special conditions being granted in this bill. Some confessed to me later that they were not very happy about guaranteeing a higher education institution a given sum in future state budgets (even if the sum in question was relatively small), and they were also uneasy about granting immunity from most state procedural controls. They believed that such controls had evolved over long periods of time and had a certain cachet of legitimate accountability to them. But, as one staff member put it, "When the governor says 'jump,' we jump!" The fact that the governor's head of the Office of Budget and Fiscal Planning was Charles Benton made the "jumping" even more certain. Benton had been well known in Annapolis for wanting to devolve more powers to operating units since his days in the 1950s representing President Curly Byrd's University of Maryland team in the state capitol arguing for more fiscal flexibility.

St. Mary's College had been so effective with its legislative relations during the years leading up to the new status bill that there was remarkably easy sailing. As I heard a legislator describe it, the St. Mary's team would establish a set of indicators by which they were willing to be evaluated and then report on these, year by year, with each year's report apparently showing progress along most dimensions (for example, SAT scores of entering freshmen, the percentage of minority students, and the number of faculty with terminal degrees). Thus, when the bill went to two Senate and three House committees, few significant problems were raised. One senator was adamant that college freedom from state building controls would apply only to building put up with private funds, and that when state tax dollars were being used, normal state controls would continue. Satisfied on this point, he voted with all other senators but one to approve the bill. Similarly in the House of Delegates, only one vote was cast against the bill.

Although the bill provided for college immunity from most state procedural controls, it specified continuing obligations to "report to the Maryland Higher Education Commission on all assessment and accountability guidelines set by the Maryland Higher Education Commission" [14–207; (A)] and furthermore required both an annual audit by an independent certified public accountant and access to college books "at any reasonable time" by the Division of Audits of the Department of Fiscal Services [14–207; (B) (2)(3)].

At a time when leaders of many other public sector institutions were singing for the most part songs of gloom and doom because of the long-range prospects of state fiscal crisis, it was evidently refreshing for state officials to find one institution that was more upbeat. And it obviously did not hurt St. Mary's' chances that it was to constitute such a small exception: with only around fifteen hundred students and more than $10 million in state funds, it was not going to tear huge holes in either the state budget or the state accountability processes if an exception were made in its case.

Perceptions of the Consequences of the Altered Status

Although the major direct consequences of going to a hybrid public-private status have probably been in the areas of claimed savings regarding procurement and capital development processes, it seems fitting to put those items in the broader context of an overall assessment of the institution. Fortunately for this study, just such an appraisal was undertaken by a ten-person Middle States accreditation team in October 1995, and their judgment was loud and clear:

St. Mary's College is a strong, healthy institution. Under excellent leadership, it has enjoyed remarkable success in establishing a new—and highly desirable—relationship with the State of Maryland and in beginning to achieve a significant level of support from private sources. With a diverse and talented student body and a faculty that is dedicated to excellent teaching, St. Mary's has become a public liberal arts college of very high quality—and a nationally recognized model in public higher education. The achievements of the College, along with its excellent facilities, dedicated faculty and enthusiastic students, sound student programs, able administration, and sense of community lead the Middle States Team to conclude that St. Mary's is ready to realize its full potential as an honors college. All these factors provide a sound base for the next step in the College's development, the full fruition of a careful planning process for the Honors College. [Middle States Association of Colleges and Schools, 1995, p. 14]

Let us examine the various dimensions of campus life, to see whether the changed status of the institution with the state has seemed to accompany (whether causing is another issue) any significant alterations in its traditional practices.

Curriculum

The Middle States Team Report offered strong praise for the careful and comprehensive planning process by which the college had prepared for the transition to a public honors college. The Reaccreditation Self-Study that St. Mary's prepared for the accreditation visit provides great detail about the arrangements for the transition and notes various problems in passing: the ways in which general education, major, and interdisciplinary emphases could be reconciled; the demands of the proposed new senior project; and the need to bring into the planning process both transfer students who would have taken their introductory work elsewhere and more recently recruited faculty who would not have participated in the earlier planning stages. The final product, passed by the faculty in 1996 after three years of widely participatory planning, reflected the institution's new status with state government in at least two major ways.

First, St. Mary's status as a public honors college (granted in 1991 prior to its special legislation) and its 1992 immunity from several traditional state procedural controls undoubtedly strengthened its case to propose innovations in its curriculum and its faculty-student relations in ways that departed from traditional state concerns about faculty workload and student credit hours. The culminating senior St. Mary's Project, worth eight academic credits, could not have been planned unless its nontraditional teaching and advising relationships had been granted more leeway by the Maryland Higher Education Commission, which still retained powers over St. Mary's assessment and accountability patterns. The Self-Study notes: "The College's designation as an honors college may provide the leverage we need to experiment with a greater variety of forms of student-faculty contact and educational activities than the State credit-hour and other guidelines can encompass" (p. 115). The public honors planning has been summarized in a brief document describing the special problems to be confronted when establishing an honors program not just for a select segment of the college's student population, but for the entire student body, and one noted for its diverse nature.

Second, the lump-sum budgeting allowed by the 1992 legislation had a dramatic effect on the nature of the academic planning. Middle-level administrators and faculty, encouraged to link five-year academic planning to realistic budget figures, ensured that the college's internal budgeting was now dealing with funds under the internal control of the college and not hypothetical budgets projected for normal state budgetary review purposes.

Students

Regarding number, diversity, and quality of incoming students, it is safe to say that all three elements were improving before the new status, but all three continued to improve afterward as well. The size of the student body has not been an issue, for the college's physical plant has a capacity for around fifteen hundred to sixteen hundred, and that figure has been easily attainable. Diversity and quality, however, are important variables, and there the record is impressive.

St. Mary's pledged to the state that its intentions to double its tuition in five years, from $2,500 to $5,000, would not be allowed to make the college into an upper-middle-class white enclave. The statistics in Table 4.1 reveal that the promise so far has been kept. The minority student percentages are even higher if one examines the statistics for entering freshmen only: 19 percent were minority, and their retention rates were marginally stronger than for the average of the entire student body (Reaccreditation Self-Study Committee, 1995, p. 19). In view of some of the stereotypes suggesting that choices must be made between quality and equality, the St. Mary's data show that quality improved at the same time that diversity increased. Combined SAT scores had increased from an average of 956 in 1983 to 1170 in 1994. High school academic course grade point average had risen from 2.85 in 1988 to 3.24 in 1994. Advanced placement credits had increased from forty-eight awarded in 1987 to seven hundred in 1994.

This combination of improving both diversity and quality was achieved in the face of doubling tuition (from about $2,500 a year) by raising the amount of institutional student aid to $1,025,000, helping five hundred students in 1995, all these in addition to student aid received from federal and Maryland state sources. The Campaign for National Prominence helped raise an additional $9 million to add to the endowment for student aid. No student admitted is turned away for lack of means to pay.

Table 4.1. Racial Composition of the Full-Time Student Body.

	African-American	Native American	Asian	Hispanic	White
FY 1994	10.6%	0.2%	3.8%	1.8%	83.5%
FY 1993	9.3	0.2	4.7	1.9	84.0
FY 1992	8.5	0.2	4.1	1.3	85.9
FY 1991	8.5	0.1	3.6	1.4	86.4

Source: Reaccreditation Self-Study Committee, 1995, p. 15.

Faculty

St. Mary's faculty during the period 1992–1996 also increased in size, diversity, and quality. Largely as a result of funds raised by the Campaign for National Prominence, the number of full-time faculty grew from 72 in 1983 to 110 in 1994, with another 54 serving part-time in 1994. The student-faculty ratio had improved from 16:1 in the late 1980s to 13.6:1 in 1994. The ultimate target is to have a 12:1 ratio, which would mean 125 full-time faculty lines for an ideal student body of 1,650.

The diversity of the faculty has increased with respect to both gender and race. The representation of women grew from 25 percent in 1983 to 36 percent in 1994, although their numbers are stronger at the subprofessor ranks; the representation of minority faculty increased from 8 percent in 1983 to 19 percent in 1994. Here too the larger numbers are in the lower and intermediate ranks.

Regarding improvements in faculty quality, the Middle States Association of Colleges and Schools Evaluation Team (1995) noted the "increasingly more effective national searches for new faculty" (p. 4). The team complimented the college on paying serious attention to excellence in teaching, but did note that although "scholarship leading to peer reviewed publication or its equivalent is respected at St. Mary's,…its relative importance is unclear" (p. 4). Each faculty member normally teaches three courses a semester.

Concerning faculty pay, the college conformed to general state policy in awarding no salary increases in the fiscal crisis years of FY 1992 and FY 1993, but later put $1.4 million into more substantial increases and then on September 6, 1995, reached agreement with a faculty committee and the faculty senate on a policy on faculty compensation. Although some faculty, like some classified staff, were reluctant to give up the COLAs that sometimes went to other state personnel, the new policy based all increases on merit evaluations.

There were provisions for an inadequate performance rating, with appeals procedures carefully described. The information given to faculty and classified staff was that more money net was being given in merit raises than would have been coming from COLAs, but its distribution was somewhat different because of the merit differentials. A faculty compensation sheet, based on the American Association of University Professors' March–April 1995 issue of

Academe, which provided salary data on nearly all U.S. colleges and universities, showed that St. Mary's salaries compared favorably to certain public sector counterparts (State University of New York at Old Westbury and at Purchase; University of Minnesota at Morris) but were generally under most of the private liberal arts colleges chosen (Bates, Carleton, Colby, Colorado, Davidson, Franklin and Marshall, Gettysburg, Hamilton, and Washington).

Nonteaching Staff

The nonteaching staff evidently believed what they had been told about compensation and the fairness of the merit evaluations because when a confidential survey was taken of employee morale in summer 1995, the results (shared with me) were on the whole gratifying to the institution and its leaders. The survey of some fifty-six items, adapted from one used at Northern Michigan University, obtained a response rate of 64 percent from the 208 full- and part-time staff. The key phrase from a detailed analysis of the results, broken down sometimes by gender and race, was that the "College can be quite proud that employees seem pretty satisfied with working conditions at the College."

Governance and Finance

Recognizing that the greater powers of self-government granted by the 1992 legislation brought heavier responsibilities to the board of trustees, the college received legislative authorization in 1994 to expand the seventeen-member board gradually to a total of twenty-five. Of the twenty members in 1995, five were women and two were African American. The board has created seven standing committees and drew the praise of the Middle States Team as an especially illustrious and hard-working body. This issue of the value of each institution having its own separate board of trustees will be revisited in the Conclusion.

Concerning finance, a Maryland higher education general fund history (Maryland Higher Education Commission, 1996) reveals that at least into FY 1997, St. Mary's College has suffered no loss in state funds by accepting the cap. This is because the additional funds to cover inflation generated by the implicit price deflator have acted to increase St. Mary's state appropriations by a percentage that compares favorably with the normal increases granted to the eleven-campus University of Maryland system during this period. The figures for St. Mary's rose 13.4 percent, from $10.4 million in FY 1993 to $11.8 million in FY 1997. For the University of Maryland system as a whole, the increase was 10.5 percent, from $525.7 million in FY 1993 to $581.1 million in FY 1997. (If we note that $225,000 of the St. Mary's four-year increase was a separate state "payback" for part of an earlier $300,000 state shortfall, then the four-year increase becomes $1.2 million, or about 11.2 percent. That smaller percentage, however, still compares favorably with the system's 10.5 percent. Also note that the 10.5 percent figure is a University of Maryland system average and that some campuses got somewhat more and some somewhat less.)

Benefits from Greater Procedural Freedoms

In a staff memorandum to President Lewis dated September 14, 1995, estimates were offered of "significant savings to the College" stemming from the autonomy legislation. Although many savings reportedly resulted from numerous relatively small purchases, "two procurements have resulted in dramatic savings...because the College has not had to get major procurements approved by multiple State offices and instead has been able to act quickly to take advantage of favorable market conditions."

The first of these concerned the construction of forty townhouses for resident students in 1993. Since these were being put up without state funds, the college was freed from state protocol for capital improvements. "The College was able to hire and begin construction on the townhouses within six months of the date our Board approved the project. Because we were able to take advantage of a tight construction market, the successful contract bid was more than a million dollars below the architect's estimate. The College realized additional savings in debt service payments because it was able to take advantage of a favorable bond market. The College's *ability to position itself, act decisively, and control the pace of construction resulted in a $2.3 million savings on a $4.7 million capital construction project*" (emphasis added).

The memorandum then related the details of a more recent 25 percent savings in the purchase of 179 multimedia computer systems. Presumably because college autonomy allowed its officers "to exploit rapid price and availability changes, rather than be bound by State procurement procedures, such as the blanket ordering agreement," a normal $480,000 order was obtained for $360,000 and, furthermore, was obtained on time, while many other higher education institutions "experienced delays in delivery of [their] computers."

When state officials responsible for procedural controls over expenditures with state dollars were confronted with these claims, their reactions tended to be of two sorts. On the one hand, there was some recognition that because of driving themes to get decisions made as close to the operating arenas as possible, the state does need to pull back somewhat from its possibly overly detailed accountability patterns. Computer purchase, for example, was cited as a specific area where the general state policies were being reconsidered, not just for higher education but for state offices in general.

On the other hand, several such officials pointed out that the short-run "good news" from St. Mary's about savings was dependent on there being "favorable market conditions" for them to take advantage of. If their greater freedoms had had to operate in deteriorating conditions, "they might not have found their liberties so intoxicating."

Conclusion

Although its procedural accountability patterns with the state have been altered, St. Mary's College's substantive accountability patterns to the Maryland Higher Education Commission (MHEC) remain. Its basic role and mission still have to be approved by MHEC; it is still subject to MHEC guidelines regarding general education requirements and student assessment procedures. It is this distinction that may mean that the St. Mary's precedent may have broader relevance for other public sector institutions.

Revisiting the 1992 Agreement

Toward the end of most of my interviews for this chapter, I asked each respondent whether, with the advantage of hindsight, he or she would have changed anything in the original agreement. The answers more often than not were negative, but a few suggestions surfaced from each side.

From the campus came the thought that if freedom from state controls worked well for capital projects put up with private funds, why would not it also work well for projects funded by tax dollars? Campus administrators contrasted the relative ease with which the privately funded townhouses had been constructed with the more complex and costly state-controlled processes needed to build the very welcome $16 million new science center.

Also mentioned by a campus official was the fact that the original 1993 state appropriation to St. Mary's, on which all subsequent appropriations were to be based, was not tied to an explicit college enrollment. Therefore, speculated this source, were state authorities later to urge the college to expand "significantly" (more than 200 above their current 1,650 target), the college would be justified in reopening the size of the basic grant.

From the state side came the concern that it was not wise to put even a small part of the state budget out of the discretionary part of the budget. With state fiscal conditions facing such uncertain state priorities, *nothing* in the budget should be sacred. At a much lesser level of impact, another state official did not think even granting the protection of the implicit price deflator was called for. There was some recognition that fewer procedural controls over higher education in general might be a good idea in certain designated areas, and the case was cited that in 1994 higher education was exempted from a statewide effort to coordinate information technology.

Given the way things have evolved since 1992, one can understand why most institutional representatives were basically satisfied with the agreement, but it was mildly surprising to find most state officials also relatively supportive. One legislator, speaking of earlier being on the receiving end of the college lobbying, did complain, "They whine a lot," but then did not take this irritation so far as to oppose the actual changes and did not later wish to alter the agreement except in one area. According to this legislator, the newly given college freedoms with respect to personnel policies still left the state with the legal responsibilities for retirement benefits. Therefore this legislator was going to keep a close eye on how St. Mary's used its personnel freedoms to make sure that the state was not presented with some fiscally awkward obligations.

Another outcome of the 1992 agreement that may not have been fully anticipated was the extent to which being given both the power and the responsibility for self-government would bring more vitality to the college governing processes. It was easier to attract outstanding persons to serve on the board of trustees when the nominees were made to understand that they were not simply figureheads; their decisions would shape the college and demonstrate its general accountability to the people of Maryland. And internally, when the faculty and administrators learned that the system of lump-sum budgeting would allow the institution to pass considerable discretion down to the spending units and that they would then become accountable for their decisions, the budgeting calculations and spending habits reportedly no longer dealt with "games with the state" but rather with real decisions showing fiscal responsibility. I have already noted how the new vitality in internal budgeting had aided the five-year academic planning for the public honors college curriculum to be linked more carefully to fiscal calculations.

State officials in the attorney general's office pointed out the caution that if ever things should go wrong in capital building projects put up with private funds, the very absence of state officials normally welcomed by the college would also mean that the college's own senior administrators would have to carry the process. So far, in the limited history of the agreement, such a situation has not arisen, so the "costs" of this freedom are not yet apparent.

Political Dimensions

One of the more politically astute members of the St. Mary's board reported that, if it had been so inclined, the University of Maryland system leadership would have been able to block the 1992 agreement. Obviously it chose not to do so, and when queried later, a university system official said that his colleagues wished St. Mary's well and hoped that the legislature would take that experience as more justification to relax their state procedural controls a bit more. Evidently some fruitful negotiations were already taking place, and it perhaps does not hurt that the governor who succeeded William Donald Schaefer was Parris Glendening, a former professor from the university's College Park campus or that his choice for secretary of higher education (and CEO of MHEC) was Patricia Florestano, a former professor and senior administrator from the university system. Furthermore, presidents of campuses within the University of Maryland system seemed supportive of the system leadership, one remarking to me that his reaction to St. Mary's special status was "more envy than hostility."

The leadership of the Maryland Independent College and University Association (the statewide association of private institutions) took no formal position on St. Mary's change in status, but privately hoped that the changes would help the institution.

It was a sign of the college's continuing good relations in the state capital that when its strong supporters, Governor Schaefer and Secretary of Higher Education Aery, left office, the new governor appointed Schaefer to the St. Mary's board of trustees and appointed Ed Clarke, former chair of the St. Mary's board, to be chair of the MHEC. Furthermore, the new secretary of higher education, Florestano, appointed as her chief deputy Michael Rosenthal, academic vice president at St. Mary's some years earlier. That no one expects the 1992 agreement to be negated soon should not be much of a surprise.

Broader Lessons Learned

Four years may be an inadequate time frame in which to try to evaluate the results of the 1992 legislation; thus, all conclusions that I present must remain tentative for the time being.

How unique is St. Mary's? Over and over again, respondents in Annapolis noted that the St. Mary's Agreement had been achieved only because, with approximately fifteen students and a state budget of around $10 million (in 1993), the college constituted such a small "exception" that its unusual status could be granted. And earlier, the particular conditions at St. Mary's that made possible taking the risks were listed: its secure market niche, its solid record on diversity, its strong board of trustees, and its increasing success in raising private funds.

Must the St. Mary's lessons remain unique to that unique institution, or is it possible to find some relevant broader meanings? President Lewis, who stepped down in summer 1996, anticipated that question and attempted an answer: "The St. Mary's College model in its entirety then, perhaps is not feasible for all public institutions. Yet within this plan, others may find certain pieces to borrow, a direction to take" (1994, p. 24).

Among the "certain pieces" he mentioned, two are particularly relevant: the great value of individual governing boards for each campus in the public sector and the possibility of the state's granting more procedural autonomy to the entire public sector. In some ways, the first may be prerequisite to the second, for the state may be reluctant to grant more procedural freedoms to an institution until it is assured that careful governance structures and procedures are there to make sure that the greater freedoms will not be abused. Trustees of a central board in vast public multicampus systems cannot spend the time to keep themselves informed in detail about the ways in which the individual institutions under their charge may or may not be using newly granted freedoms wisely and carefully. Clearly the message here is that a board for each campus is the better way to go. But such a pattern is rare in state public sectors; more often than not, states have either several multicampus system boards under a coordinating board, or all public four-year institutions (and sometimes the public two-year colleges as well) are under one consolidated governing board. It is true that some consolidated governing boards (for example, North Carolina) and some multicampus system governing boards (for example, Maryland) have allowed the establishment of local advisory boards, but whether high-quality appointments would accept service on local boards that are advisory only and exist at the pleasure of the central governing board remains to be seen.

In the eleven-campus University of Maryland system, eight campuses have created a local board of visitors in accordance with the guidelines laid down by the system's board of regents: Bowie State; Frostburg State; Towson State; University of Baltimore; University of Maryland at Baltimore (UMAB); University of Maryland, Baltimore County; University of Maryland, College Park; and University of Maryland, University College. One of these campuses, UMAB, the medical and law school campus, citing a precedent from Oregon where a public medical campus had been privatized, has considered withdrawing from the university system and creating a not-for-profit corporation, as its hospital did thirteen years ago. Such a change would require state approval (*Baltimore Sun*, Dec.

11, 1995). On the premise that half a loaf is better than none, I urge the appointment of even advisory local boards, but with the additional exhortation that they then negotiate to acquire as many devolved powers as possible.

The second Lewis piece referred to greater autonomy for public sector institutions. Here the distinction between procedural and substantive autonomy becomes crucial, for it is argued that the state's public interest can be well protected with a public sector whose substantive goals and programs are shared with the state through what has been called a "suitably sensitive mechanism" (for example, a state coordinating board) (Berdahl, 1971, p. 15) but where the state yields the broadest array of procedural freedoms to the institutions. If state controls over line-item budgeting, personnel policies, procurement policies, and building procedures are found more often than not to result in bureaucratic delays and additional costs (as the St. Mary's case suggests that they do), then enlightened members of the state executive and legislative branches should recognize that procedural accountability is a means rather than an end in itself. If more efficient and more effective delivery of public services can be obtained by cutting back state procedural controls, it should be done for as many of the public sector institutions as state authorities judge to have the internal administrative capacities to use those freedoms wisely and well. Although such a policy would undoubtedly escalate political controversy in that some public institutions might be granted more procedural freedom than others, presumably it would also act as the best incentive system for the other institutions to improve their administrative procedures in order to qualify for the granting of more flexibility.

Although some discussions of privatization in the public sector have referred to allowing units such as a medical school to operate as an independent function, determining its own mission, setting its own tuition, hiring its own faculty and staff, fixing its own salaries, and so on, that form of privatization raises problems. Both procedural and substantive controls have been surrendered. To my thinking, the state should retain a partnership role in the substantive goals and programs to ensure that the public interest is being served. Therefore, I endorse the different form of privatization seen in the St. Mary's case, where the college continues its obligations to the MHEC for approval of its role and mission and for reports dealing with student assessments and general education, but nevertheless uses its sweeping powers of self-government in procedural domains to improve its academic quality, maintain broad student access, and raise more funds through increased efforts in the private market.

An important variable in the success of St. Mary's, which was omitted in President Lewis's article (for obvious reasons of his modesty), was the crucial role of the president himself. Organization theory texts are filled with debates as to whether presidents make a difference or whether they are like interchangeable light bulbs. While St. Mary's is much too small an institution for me to make larger claims based on its experiences, I could not end this essay without remarking on the obvious impact President Lewis had on the institution in his thirteen years in office. Faculty, staff, and students were understandably concerned as President Lewis retired in the summer of 1996, hoping that his successor, Maggie O'Brien, former president of Hollins College in Virginia, will have a good appetite for fundraising and for continuing the charmed Lewis touch in recruitment of outstanding board members.

Chapter Five

Defining the Scope and Limits of Autonomy: New Jersey

Darryl G. Greer

New Jersey higher education has achieved a significant amount of autonomy from state government since the mid-1980s. No other state has as consistently and explicitly decentralized and deregulated governance and coordination of its public colleges and universities. The New Jersey experience with institutional self-governance evolves from an explicit public policy decision to provide institutions with greater autonomy over their affairs in order to strengthen educational diversity, excellence, and accountability. The ultimate test of the New Jersey experience will not be higher education's ability to survive in a deregulated world but its capacity to use its new freedom to become more diverse and better.

In 1994, dramatic abolition of the state Board and Department of Higher Education (BHE/DHE), a cabinet-level agency applying strong regulatory authority, particularly over the nine state colleges, allowed for substantially greater autonomy. The 1994 Higher Education Restructuring Act further decentralized authority to local boards of trustees, creating a nonregulatory, state-level coordinating body—the Commission on Higher Education—as well as a statewide Presidents' Council. The new structure requires presidents of all public and private institutions, and representatives of proprietary ones, to assist in coordinating higher education. The key policy principle driving the autonomy movement and restructuring law asserts that quality, educational service, innovation, and accountability are more likely to be upheld through policy set by local boards of trustees rather than through a centralized state bureaucracy.

This chapter explores in detail the New Jersey experience with autonomy and offers conclusions regarding the distinctions between administrative or operational and policy autonomy, autonomy's impact on relationships with political leaders, strengths and weaknesses under autonomous governance, and prospects for the future.

The New Jersey Context

New Jersey is a richly diverse state that often is better known by its turnpike exit numbers than by its abundant natural resources and distinctive institutions of higher education. Characterized by a densely populated northern tier and a more sparsely populated, rural and farm-dominated southern portion, the Garden State has a population of 7.5 million and is among the most ethnically diverse states in the nation. As one of the richest states, New Jersey has generously supported higher education. The state ranks among the top ten in total spending for higher education, appropriating about $1.2 billion annually. Total operating budgets for the state's public colleges and universities exceed $3 billion each year.

New Jersey nevertheless lagged compared to other states in investing in a strong public higher education structure. Rutgers University became the state's first public university only in 1956. No state medical school or engineering and technology university existed until the 1960s. The state colleges remained teachers' colleges until the mid-1970s.

Currently the higher education enterprise consists of three public research universities (Rutgers University, the New Jersey Institute of Technology, and the University of Medicine and Dentistry of New Jersey), nine state colleges or universities, fourteen independent colleges or universities, and nineteen community colleges, as well as several proprietary and religious institutions. Collectively these institutions enroll about 340,000 students, placing

New Jersey twelfth nationally in total students enrolled in higher education. Significantly, 25 percent of this enrollment consists of ethnic and racial minorities.

The state colleges serve as the state's principal baccalaureate institutions, graduating about 40 percent of new baccalaureate holders annually. They enroll approximately 78,000 undergraduate and graduate students.

Historically, the independent college sector, distinguished by Princeton University, has enjoyed a close relationship with state government. New Jersey's Independent College Aid Act, enacted in 1972, provides direct appropriations to private colleges, totaling roughly $20 million annually. Furthermore, these institutions receive significant capital monies for upgrading facilities and equipment, as well as over $45 million annually provided by New Jersey's generous student financial aid programs.

The state ranks among the top five in student financial aid programs nationally, providing nearly $150 million each year in tuition assistance, merit grants, and opportunity grants. The significant investment in student aid, and through grants in particular, has helped keep college in New Jersey affordable, even as public college tuition rates doubled between 1985 and 1995.

Although the state appropriations for higher education funding in New Jersey doubled during the 1980s, higher education services as a share of total state appropriations declined to 11.7 percent from 13.5 percent. During the 1990s, state investment has dropped further. Tuition has grown as a share of total college revenue; whereas the state paid for about 70 percent of instructional costs in 1989, direct state appropriations currently cover about 60 percent of these costs. Tuition at the state colleges is substantial, ranging between $2,600 and $3,500 per year.

As in many other states with mature higher education structures, New Jersey faces the dilemma of maintaining access, quality, and affordability during a time of diminishing state resources. Tax cuts, slow revenue growth, and increased state spending mandates for K–12 education, health care, and corrections have left higher education with a diminished share of the pie.

Two conflicting aspects of the political culture of New Jersey are especially relevant to this story of deregulation: strong local governments and a powerful labor movement. Local autonomy, or home rule, is the political norm in New Jersey, as reflected in its municipal-based local government and roughly six hundred independently governed school districts. Thus, decentralization is generally regarded as a good thing by many citizens. In contrast, strong labor unions have worked against decentralization and local campus autonomy. Unionized faculty exercise substantial political influence and often oppose the initiatives of local governing boards, as well as college presidents. Opposition of the state college faculty union to greater authority for campus trustees and presidents continues to influence and restrict decentralization in the state.

The Coordinating Board

In 1966 New Jersey created and subsequently maintained its coordinating board for the same reasons as other states instituted these regulatory agencies: to control the growth and direction of public institutions, mediate between the growing public sector and the state's strong private colleges and universities, and license schools for federal financial aid purposes. Most states experienced some level of tension between the coordinating board and the institutions; the conflict reached higher levels in the Garden State than elsewhere.

Several factors contributed to this unusually high level of conflict. From the start, the Department of Higher Education exercised both coordinating and governing responsibilities. Thus, in addition to coordinating statewide planning and program approval, for example, the chancellor also strongly influenced the selection of presidents at the state colleges, controlled tuition rates, and played a formal role in naming local college trustees. Local college leaders found this massive exercise of authority irksome.

The same law that created the coordinating board also created its nemesis, local boards of trustees for each of the nine state colleges. These institutional advocates chafed under the rule of the coordinating agency and its chancellors. The local boards attempted repeatedly to pass legislation that would strengthen their authority while restricting that of the Department of Higher Education (DHE). Nearly thirty years after their creation, these groups were successful in acquiring much of the authority they sought.

Finally, it cannot be denied that the personal leadership style of the department's executive, especially Chancellor T. Edward Hollander, contributed to an atmosphere of conflict. Hollander was a tough-minded administrator unafraid to use the considerable power of his office. Critics described him as abrasive and authoritarian, lacking the diplomatic style that enabled other state higher education executives to manage the inevitable disagreements between the central authority and the campuses.

In response to what it regarded as the overweening authority of the DHE, the state legislature enacted in 1969 the first State College Autonomy Law, vesting broad authority over the state colleges with boards of trustees. Nevertheless, it failed to achieve its purpose, as state agencies invoked statutory authority over the colleges and continued to control financial, academic, and personnel matters at the institutions.

In matters of personnel, for example, the colleges were subject to the same civil service regulations governing all state employees. The State Office of Employee Relations controlled collective bargaining. The DHE and a state purchasing and property division managed in large measure the purchase of goods and services, and the state Division of Building and Construction controlled construction at the institutions. Although the State College Autonomy Law tempered the authority of these state agencies in theory, in practice state control remained strong for another decade.

Increasing Autonomy and Conflict

Prompted by college presidents' and trustees' strong advocacy and recommendations of various commissions favoring greater autonomy, the governor and legislature enacted the 1986 State College Autonomy Law. This law followed similar legislation proposed a year earlier, which had failed to pass in the face of strong union opposition. By shifting authority to trustees from government, the law sought to improve academic quality and diversity, provide greater prestige for the state colleges, and increase local accountability for financial affairs, operations, and personnel management.

The 1986 State College Autonomy Law focused fundamentally on providing the state colleges with explicit operational autonomy. The statute granted much greater authority to the campuses over administrative matters, such as purchasing and contracting, revenue, payroll, budget, and facilities management. Significantly, for the first time, it granted boards of trustees authority to set tuition and fees, thereby paving the way for differential tuition policy and further mission differentiation. The law also gave boards of trustees full authority over hiring and compensating college presidents without DHE regulation, and gave the trustees and presidents greater authority over personnel policy decisions governing faculty and professional staff hiring, promotion, and compensation.

Promises of greater policy autonomy on tuition, facilities, construction, labor negotiations, and legal counsel, however, remained unfulfilled. The DHE and other cabinet bureaucracies continued to oppose vesting full policy authority with the campuses. For example, under the 1986 State College Autonomy Law, each college board of trustees was to set tuition independently from the state. However, the DHE used an ill-defined authority to impose tuition guidelines as a means of regulating campus tuition policy. It turned such guidelines into an indirect means of forcing colleges to request exemptions from a tuition ceiling. Tension spilled over publicly when some trustee boards balked at adhering to these guidelines.

Although campus boards had the authority in law to acquire and dispose of real property, several state bureaucracies restricted them from exercising this authority. The colleges still needed the approval of five or more state agencies for each construction project. And although they were supposedly in control of purchasing directly, they still were required to follow a time-consuming state competitive bid procedure.

In two key policy areas—personnel and legal representation—the gap between autonomy promised in law but not accomplished in practice increased conflict between colleges and the state. The autonomy statutes bestowed trustee boards with authority over personnel policies governing faculty and staff but not over clerical and maintenance staff employees. Nor did the law grant colleges authority for negotiating labor contracts with their unionized staff. The governor remained the employer of record. The state, not the colleges, would continue to negotiate contracts with public sector labor unions on behalf of the colleges. This division of authority exacerbated college financial problems when state government failed to fund the salary increases it had negotiated.

The autonomy law also failed to allow the colleges to retain their own legal counsel. With increased trustee responsibility and potential liability for decisions, the state attorney general remained the attorney of record for the campuses. This situation often resulted in ineffective legal advocacy, since the attorney general represented both the colleges and the agencies of government seeking to retain policy control over them.

One final shortcoming of the law was that it retained the chancellor's involvement in appointing trustees to the state colleges. By the end of the 1980s, several colleges, especially Trenton State College (renamed in 1996 the College of New Jersey), had applied their recently won autonomy to expand programs, build new facilities, and raise tuition to pay for growth as state resources diminished. The DHE continued to use trustee appointments as a carrot or stick to influence these campus policy decisions.

Ironically, greater college autonomy created greater resentment toward remaining state control. Greater autonomy for campus trustee boards not only heightened expectations for making decisions free of government, but also led to a greater realization of how continuing state regulation inhibited freedom to act. As some of the colleges used their expanded autonomy, for example, to raise tuition or to create new programs, state government responded as it had historically: looking to the DHE to manage the negative political consequences of such actions. Intense disagreements developed over mission expansion, trustee appointments, tuition, facilities, and labor policy. Many state college presidents and trustees believed these conflicts could not be remedied without eliminating the DHE.

Advocates for Autonomy

Given the intense opposition of the faculty union, the key factors for the success of the colleges in getting the law passed were gubernatorial leadership and an alliance of governing boards.

Study commissions provided rationales for greater autonomy, and college leaders had learned from their earlier mistakes. Vague statutory assurances of autonomy, without the transfer of specific authorities to back up such promises, were unreliable. Thus, the 1986 law was more specific. But most important, Governor Thomas Kean's public support contributed to the successful enactment of the 1986 State College Autonomy Law. For the governor, autonomy, coupled with incentive funding, was a means of improving the quality and scope of higher education.

Another important aspect of the 1986 success was structural. The colleges needed a strong advocate. In 1985, college presidents and trustees had led a drive to create in law the New Jersey State College Governing Boards Association, Inc. (GBA), replacing the advisory Council of State Colleges that had been under DHE purview. The GBA, as a nongovernmental, nonprofit organization, would be funded and governed by the colleges themselves. Today, as a nonprofit organization, GBA provides policy research and advocacy on all matters affecting the state colleges and advises the governor and legislature regarding public policy affecting the colleges. The association played a central role in higher education restructuring.

The governor and legislature viewed the association as a means of balancing the powerful influence of statewide unions, which opposed autonomy. Many observers believed the faculty union in particular represented a major stumbling block to effective shared governance and academic leadership at the colleges. For example, the union supported DHE regulation of faculty promotion and tenure, and salary policy. Such regulation forced the colleges into uniform practices, thereby inhibiting their differential strategic development. Greater trustee and presidential authority, especially in areas of finance and personnel, were by definition a threat to maintaining statewide union influence. The GBA immediately became a strong countervailing force to the union and to the DHE.

Policies and Coordination

In the late 1980s and early 1990s relationships between the state colleges and the DHE continued to deteriorate. Declining state investment in higher education was coupled with increasing pressure on the campuses to exercise greater autonomy to manage their limited resources effectively. To help offset state budget reductions, campuses called for increased tuition and fees. The resulting tension exacerbated disagreements over tuition policy, new academic programs, and facilities. As a member of the governor's cabinet, the chancellor, by circumstance and by choice, found himself in the difficult position of promoting policy that protected the governor from criticism from college constituencies over budget cuts. He also attempted to engage college presidents and trustees in collaborating on total quality improvement and cost reductions, all the while continuing to include a contentious faculty union in state college policy consultations.

The DHE's attempts to balance this difficult political agenda placed it, the colleges, and the union at greater odds. In effect, the DHE undermined one of its primary purposes by politicizing higher education policy at the state level. Some colleges, such as the College of New Jersey (TCNJ), Montclair, and Rowan, prepared to extend their missions by adding new professional or doctoral programs. Declining state appropriations and the growing ambitions of these colleges created within the higher education community new tensions over turf.

TCNJ, for example, pushed autonomy to its limits by proposing a new engineering program that would compete with existing programs in other public colleges. The college wrangled publicly with the DHE for over two years to win approval for the program. The fight, which dragged in the governor and legislators, often moved away from the program's merits, disintegrating into a political clash between the authority of the board of trustees and that of the chancellor, characterized by the chancellor's openly questioning the college's mission. A similar highly visible battle raged for several years over that same college's decision to provide certain faculty and administrators with campus-owned housing as a condition of employment. These controversies further undermined the coordinating board's reputation for leadership.

The Whitman Initiative

After a lackluster start in her gubernatorial campaign in 1993, candidate Christine Todd Whitman proposed a major rollback in state income and other taxes, juxtaposed with Governor Jim Florio's record of steep tax increases early in his first term. This issue, more than any other one, gave the Whitman campaign victory. Whitman also pledged to reduce the burden of government on citizens through restructuring and deregulation. Higher education was not a major campaign issue for either candidate.

Governor Whitman moved quickly to implement her campaign promises. In January 1994, she announced a plan to roll back the state income tax by 30 percent in her first term, beginning with a 15 percent reduction in the first year. Plans for reinventing government through restructuring and streamlining followed soon after.

David Kehler, a newly appointed senior staff member in the treasurer's office, began a series of confidential discussions with the executive director of the GBA and the president of TCNJ to conceptualize a deregulated, decentralized structure. In contrast with New Jersey history, a study commission to justify the merits of the proposal followed, rather than preceded, the political decision.

In her March 1994 budget address, the new governor astonished most educators, legislators, reporters, and especially the chancellor and BHE by announcing her firm intention to abolish the DHE and replace it in three months with a new, decentralized structure empowering local trustee boards.

Within weeks of this bold announcement, Governor Whitman established a fifteen–member Advisory Panel on Higher Education Restructuring and charged it with determining a suitable alternate coordinating structure. The panel had wide latitude to invent a structure while holding firm on four key principles:

1. Higher education must be affordable, accessible, and of high quality.
2. Institutions require greater autonomy with a minimum of bureaucratic controls.
3. The new structure must guard against political intrusion.
4. Appropriate coordination should be provided by the state and the institutions themselves.

In May 1994, the panel, concurring with the governor that the DHE/BHE was no longer needed, proposed strengthening the authority of campus governing boards by replacing the old structure with a smaller, largely nonregulatory coordinating agency without cabinet rank, the Commission on Higher Education (CHE). It also proposed creating the New Jersey Presidents' Council (PC) to oversee academic program review and interinstitutional cooperation (Advisory Panel on Higher Education Restructuring, 1994).

The unique aspect of the new governance structure clearly is creation of the statewide presidents' coordinating council, consisting of all segments of New Jersey higher education. Whereas several states, such as Ohio and Michigan, have long-standing voluntary coordinating councils of public university presidents, no other state has created an advisory and coordinating body of presidents with formal responsibilities for coordination on budget and academic program matters such as the one in New Jersey.

The new structure of higher education stripped away layers of regulation and clarified trustee authority over legal counsel, tuition and fees, academic program approval, personnel, facilities construction, and trustee nomination. It eliminated many elements of state-level budget and academic program review and approval.

The panel recommended that institutions' boards of trustees be authorized to do the following:

- Determine board size and composition
- Nominate potential board members for the governor's consideration and appointment
- Administer personnel policies and appeals
- Exercise final authority on internal academic decisions within the scope of institutional mission
- Set tuition and fees
- Invest institutional funds
- Retain legal counsel of choice
- Control all institutional planning, financing, staffing, program offerings, and capital improvements
- Provide for public accountability for institutional performance and effective management

The advisory panel recommended, and the legislature ultimately endorsed, reevaluation of the need for numerous regulations affecting the campuses, especially those related to personnel matters. The panel also called on the new CHE to study and recommend whether the state colleges should have authority over labor negotiations, including the option to negotiate campus by campus, as is the case at state research universities and county colleges.

Opponents and Proponents of the Legislation

The legislative plan to restructure, generally supported by higher educators, and especially the state colleges, had its share of opponents and skeptics. The debate over restructuring took a strong partisan tenor (Greer and Shelly, 1995). Some Democrats accused the Republican governor of purposefully dismantling higher education coordination in order to force budget cuts, reduce student financial aid, and deny access to disadvantaged students. Although budget cuts have been forthcoming, largely because of deep tax cuts, access, opportunity, and student aid programs have remained unchanged.

The former chancellor expressed concerns that a plan adapted from other state coordinating frameworks might not work in New Jersey (Hollander, 1994). Others, including Chancellor Goldberg and the state college faculty union, warned that restructuring would result in a sacrifice of academic freedom, erode college access and affordability, increase political interference, result in fewer appropriated higher education dollars, and lead to cutthroat institutional competition.

The National Association for the Advancement of Colored People (NAACP) and advocates for economically disadvantaged students argued that trustees were likely to act irresponsibly on admissions and tuition policy, thereby threatening access and affordability. Furthermore, restructuring opponents insisted that higher education policy advocacy would be doomed without the cabinet-level status of the coordinating agency.

Proponents of the law maintained that institutions would reap greater flexibility through the elimination of unnecessary and duplicative regulation; such flexibility would lead to greater strategic policy coherence regarding mission accomplishment and therefore to greater accountability for college outcomes. Finally, they argued that decentralization, by granting presidents responsibility for statewide coordination, would provide the colleges with a better chance to build a context and constituency for advocating the value of higher education.

Convinced the restructuring law would not diminish opportunity and access to college, the governor stood up to the strong opposition from the chancellor, the BHE, civil rights activists, unions, and the state's largest daily newspaper, the *Star Ledger.* Her resolve, and the support of the overwhelming majority of her party in both legislative houses, helped to ensure legislative enactment.

Debate in the legislature over the goals of restructuring led to many compromises, including provisions mandating nearly one dozen studies and reports to be made to the governor and legislature on matters such as funding, student financial aid, labor relations, and educational outcomes. Proposals to grant colleges eminent domain and full control over disposition of property were modified to maintain state control. The legislators deferred the decision over decentralizing labor negotiations. Furthermore, the new law required annual accountability reports from the campuses and interim reports on the success of restructuring to be provided to the governor and legislature within two years (1996) and again following five years (1999) of experience with the new structure. With these and other changes, Governor Whitman signed into law the Higher Education Restructuring Act on June 23, 1994.

A Progress Report

If the deregulated system of higher education in New Jersey has not become the unmitigated disaster predicted by its critics, it has not yet fulfilled all the promises held out for deregulation or shown that the self-regulatory powers of the PC and the commission are up to the task of truly coordinating a set of largely independent institutions. Following is a report on progress in the key areas of program review, employee relations, campus management, tuition policy, legal affairs, and diversity of the student body (New Jersey Commission on Higher Education, 1996).

Academic Program Review

The new academic program peer review process requires campuses to circulate new program proposals statewide. By law, campus trustees have final authority to approve new academic programs that are within the mission. CHE/PC review is required only when a new program exceeds the college mission or is unduly costly or duplicative. The interim report of the CHE/PC on restructuring cites the establishment of seventy-three new degree programs (twenty-three associate, eighteen baccalaureate, thirty-one master's, and one doctoral), without state-level or campus controversy, since the academic program review committee was established in August 1994. The absence of conflict stands in stark contrast to the chronic battles between the colleges and the DHE, although it also suggests that the programs may not have received intense scrutiny.

A major accountability showdown may be on the horizon over new doctoral programs at state colleges. At the heart of this matter is conflict between the state colleges and research universities on mission boundaries. As the state colleges are expanding, some universities want to maintain their hegemony at the graduate level to ensure quality, enrollments, and budget support. Similarly, tension is rising among some two-year colleges and state colleges over transfer and articulation practices. It is too soon to tell if the new structure has the integrity to resolve these matters effectively, or whether some institutions will outmaneuver others to get their way. Although most campus presidents report that decentralizing program review makes sense, some critics nevertheless are concerned the programs will proliferate in the absence of strong control external to the campuses.

Employee Relations

There has been little progress in granting state college and university campuses more control over their principal cost area, personnel. Due to the political power of statewide unions, the Whitman administration has been slow in forwarding legislation freeing the colleges from remaining civil service regulation of some employees and state control over labor negotiations.

Campus-Level Management

Restructuring seems to be working better on the campus level. Many administrators report that with less bureaucratic regulation under restructuring and fewer corresponding paperwork requirements, they are better able to focus on campus initiatives such as fundraising, investments, cost controls, and long-term planning. Trustees have been especially active in exercising their authority. With clear responsibility for authoritative decisions on budget and programs, they are making decisions that effectively link personnel, budget, private giving, facilities, and tuition policy with their strategic goals. For example, Rowan, Montclair, Trenton, and Ramapo have been highly successful in increasing private giving to their colleges. Rowan has accelerated implementation of its strategic plan to initiate a new engineering school. Several institutions have applied their new authority over tuition and personnel to manage state funding cuts, hire new faculty in high-priority areas, and outsource some services such as food services and energy management.

Facilities construction approval has been streamlined by eliminating duplicative approval of the BHE and campus trustees. Millions of dollars of new construction have been put to bid and contracted without mishap or loss of public accountability.

Removing the chancellor from the boards of trustees does not appear to have adversely affected trustee accountability. Several institutions have taken advantage of the law's flexibility to increase trustee board size, augment the board talent pool, and allow for more work to be done at the committee level. Colleges report more actively pursuing trustee appointments, with both the governor and Senate, and providing more clarity about trustee responsibilities. Overall, there has been moderate improvement in the timeliness of appointments with the demise of the old structure.

Risk taking and controversial decisions are part of autonomy too. Some critics cited the name change of the College of New Jersey from Trenton State College, which created a highly visible public conflict with Princeton University, as an example of how trustees may act irresponsibly absent a stronger state-level check. On the other hand, college leaders argue that restructuring helped stave off political interference in what was a strategic marketing decision related to the college's core academic mission.

Tuition Policy

The colleges are required to hold public hearings on proposed tuition increases. To some degree, placing tuition authority squarely on the campuses has helped to depoliticize the process, making clearer the relationship between state funding and charges to students. Students seem to appreciate this new facet of restructuring. They attend hearings and regularly express their views. As full participants in the campus dialogue, they have come to understand more clearly the relationship of tuition revenues to educational quality. At many campuses, students have openly supported tuition increases.

During the new structure's first fiscal year, 1995–1996, a small appropriations increase of about 1 percent for all institutions and increases in student aid resulted in tuition increases in the range of 4 to 6 percent. In 1996–1997 budget cuts of about 3 percent led to tuition increases ranging from 5 to 10 percent.

Although New Jersey has a history of differential tuition set by local boards of trustees, perhaps no other single issue will be as volatile as tuition rates in rallying public opinion on the effectiveness of the new autonomy. It is interesting to note the highest tuition increases in recent history (10 to 15 percent) were in effect during the early 1990s, a period of budget austerity combined with strong BHE regulation. It is expected that critics of restructuring, especially minority-party legislators, will use trustee tuition decisions as a test of the deregulated system. Tax reductions, leading to deeper cuts in college appropriations, all but guarantee that tuition will increase, as will the controversy over who should bear the costs for public higher education.

Legal Affairs

The institutions appear to benefit from the ability to appoint, in a timely manner, independent counsel, while maintaining a close relationship with the attorney general on legal matters in which the attorney general has traditionally played a strong role in assisting the colleges—for example, labor dispute resolution and real property matters. Although some cost has shifted to the colleges, most college leaders are pleased to be able to seek independent legal advice.

Student Diversity

Some critics had charged that deregulation would reduce New Jersey's long-term commitment to ethnic diversity, and, in fact, the state NAACP actively opposed the 1994 reform on these grounds. These fears have proved unfounded to date. Minority enrollment has continued to grow as a percentage of total enrollment since the time of deregulation.

Statewide Planning, Coordination, and Advocacy

Although presidents, board members, and commissioners are generally pleased with their newfound independence, it remains to be seen if the two new overarching structures—the Commission on Higher Education and the Presidents' Council—can successfully work together to plan, coordinate, and make the case for public higher education. The CHE staff size of twenty-one appears adequate and has completed nearly all studies mandated by law. In retrospect, too many studies were mandated. It is clear that a nascent organization seeking to organize itself, define its mission, and build its legitimacy needed more focus. The commission must move beyond these legislative mandates to shape its own long-term policy research and advocacy agenda together with the PC.

The PC was fortunate to have the president of Rutgers, the state's most comprehensive university, as its first chair for 1994–1996. The community benefited from access to the talent pool at Rutgers, whose personnel literally acted as staff to the PC. But it is unrealistic for the PC to pin its hopes for the future on the expectation that individual institutions will provide adequate staff. The council needs a small, professional staff, as envisioned by the governor's study panel and the law.

The PC faces major tests in maintaining the integrity of the academic program review process, managing growing competition between community colleges and vocational-technical schools over programs and funding, and coordinating independent state and county colleges as each seeks state financial support. A permanent staff might help to resolve these thorny issues, but the individual presidents must show they can suppress institutional interests for the common good.

So far, institutions have cooperated through the PC on state budget development and advocacy. The colleges and universities developed a unified and credible budget policy statement for fiscal 1997. Tax cuts, however, have left the institutions with far fewer state resources than they requested.

Tensions remain, as they did under the old structure, over dedicated funding, or "earmarks," for institutions. Naturally, if lobbying for such earmarks becomes widespread during a time of reduced overall state investment, it will be difficult to sustain a unified front on the budget. So far, however, most presidents view the ability to communicate about the budget directly to the state treasurer and the governor's office as positive.

The absence of a long-term rationale for higher education funding, one of the failings of the old structure, could threaten the current harmony in this new educational community. After two years, neither the CHE nor the PC has developed a broad-based, long-term plan for advocacy of higher education. Although discussions on the topic are under way, the inability of the CHE and PC to play a strong advocacy role in the short term represents a structural defect that must be overcome.

The PC's decision to combine the functions of accountability reporting and advocacy under a single committee holds promise. This advocacy committee, along with the external relations staff from each higher education sector, has championed student financial aid, for example, without the dire consequences predicted by restructuring opponents. Both the CHE and PC are making serious efforts to communicate to the public. A series of advocacy publications directed at different constituencies such as employers and legislators are in progress. The CHE has assembled a useful, thorough report reflecting a wealth of data on the institutions and educational outcomes. Whether this kind of publicity influences public regard for higher education remains to be seen.

To date, the CHE and the PC have not worked effectively together. The commission has been reluctant to provide either strong, independent policy research or play the traditional role of buffering the institutions from political intrusion. It took the CHE two years to complete a higher education master plan that may serve as a foundation for strong advocacy and policy coordination. Many college leaders expressed displeasure with the planning process and the plan's lack of vision. To lay the blame for this unsatisfactory result on the commission alone is unfair. Had there been greater involvement from PC members and the support of a professional staff, there would likely have been fewer problems with the commission's draft plan.

Finally, proposed budget cuts, further tax reductions, and K–12 funding requirements have overshadowed the governor's occasional endorsements of higher education's value. For restructuring to succeed, the governor—who was narrowly reelected in 1997—as the initiator of this reform, needs to continue to champion the importance of higher education and her expectations for restructuring. In the absence of such visible leadership, the state's press, the public, and legislators will wonder whether restructuring is viable and whether the dire predictions of opponents regarding the failure of self-regulation might prove true.

Tensions over Accountability and Control

One of the by-products of restructuring is that higher education in New Jersey has become a flatter, less hierarchical enterprise, with all institutions participating more equitably in state-level accountability. This is not necessarily a plus for some sectors. For example, as appropriations drop, the independent colleges, which receive direct appropriations for instruction, facilities, and substantial student financial aid monies, are under greater pressure from the state treasury to account for their investment of public monies. It is interesting that a former chancellor and opponent of deregulation predicted that the "treasurer will become *de facto* the new chancellor of higher education" (Hollander, 1994, p. B2). A strong push by government to reduce support for the independent colleges and to raise expectations for accountability reporting could splinter the higher education community should independent colleges conclude their interests are at odds with those of the public colleges and universities.

Lessons Learned

The shift toward a more decentralized, deregulated, and autonomous public higher education in New Jersey has evolved over several decades, culminating in the dramatic restructuring law of 1994. Although the New Jersey case is unique, it offers several general lessons.

Restructuring Does Not Eliminate Politics

Restructuring in New Jersey did not eliminate the politics of higher education, but it did significantly change the locus of decision making away from state bureaucracy to college leaders (Education Commission of the States, 1995). The politicization of the old regulatory coordinating board, as much as any other single event, helped justify to the governor and many in the higher education community the need to restructure. The interests of the governor and legislature in higher education policy, especially funding, remain strong. But contrary to many predictions, without a central bureaucracy to act as a vehicle for political intrusion, there appears to be less rather than more political influence. The governor and legislature, for example, have fewer means beyond the appropriations act to intervene in academic decisions. If they do, they are more likely to be criticized publicly for such actions because of the presumed independence of the institutions.

Educational Principles Are Important to Reform

Although Governors Kean and Whitman played leading roles in restructuring in New Jersey, educational principles shaping restructuring goals are much more likely to come from higher education than from state government. Presidents and trustees should be ready to lead in describing the "high road" principles of self-governance. The educational principles driving restructuring in New Jersey, such as the importance of mission differentiation and quality improvement, came from college leaders. It is doubtful that legitimacy for restructuring, especially in the face of opposition, can be sustained without an explicit set of educational principles on which change is justified.

Successful Deregulation Requires Clear Purposes and Plans

Before taking steps toward fundamental deregulation of higher education governance, states and their systems should distinguish between administrative autonomy providing campuses with greater operational flexibility, such as managing budgets, purchasing, and contracting, and policy autonomy over matters such as tuition, academic programs, facilities construction, and legal counsel.

Greater administrative independence for efficiency probably will be easier to achieve in the short term than will be the more ambitious policy of autonomy for qualitative improvement. Whichever direction a state decides to take, the purpose of reforming practices or policies needs to be at the center of public policy decisions (Schick and others, 1992).

Where overlapping authorities of many state agencies exist, colleges should anticipate the need to accommodate competing interests. Whatever types of autonomy are granted should be explicit and unambiguous in order to avoid conflict and to hold both colleges and the state accountable.

A clear implementation plan accompanying the 1986 State College Autonomy Law outlined specifically which administrative functions (such as payroll, purchasing, revenue, budget, and personnel management) would be transferred from the state to the colleges. This implementation strategy, following the decision to codify these matters in law, became a means by which both the colleges and state government could hold one another accountable for change.

Moreover, the state colleges consistently set, along with government, reasonable objectives to be achieved based on the principle of improving educational diversity, quality, and greater accountability through the autonomy they gained. Such achievements have been documented through special annual reports by both the campuses and their statutory advocacy and policy research arm, the GBA (New Jersey State College Governing Boards Association, 1991). For example, special efforts were made to provide both legislative finance and education policy committees with information about outcomes of deregulation.

Deregulation Creates a Need for New Coordinating Structures

New structures will be necessary to support decentralization. The Commission on Higher Education and the Presidents' Council are two new elements. Although predating the 1994 law, the State College Governing Boards Association is a third. This association has emerged not only as the principal public voice about the state colleges, but also as a visible public policy advocate for higher education generally. It has become an important "systems maintenance" organization, filling the information and coordination void left by the elimination of a state-level regulation. Its function in organizational terms is that of aggregating interests among the colleges and articulating such interests between the campuses and state government and the broader public in order to develop and accomplish public policy.

Although the GBA has gained legitimacy as an advocate and policy adviser, its mission, dependent on intercampus cooperation, becomes more difficult as the colleges become more differentiated and independent. The common agenda becomes more difficult to define as each college gains greater freedom to pursue particular goals independent of the others.

While other states have such organizations informally, New Jersey has formally institutionalized such entities for public multicampus segments of higher education (state colleges and county colleges). Other states contemplating autonomy initiatives should consider creating such policy-facilitating organizations, the emergence of which was forecast over a decade ago (Millett, 1984).

The Good Effects of Deregulation May Be a Long Time Coming

Even with an explicit set of goals and implementation strategy, the status quo is difficult to change. Substantial momentum is built into any system of higher education, at both the state and campus levels. As the New Jersey example illustrates, the state colleges experienced several failed attempts at winning greater autonomy, even following passage of law.

Behaviors and attitudes, as well as laws and regulations, have to change in order to achieve goals. Although restructuring abolished a large cabinet-level regulatory bureaucracy and replaced it with a smaller, less regulatory, coordinating agency, the results have been far from dramatic. The new coordinating board has been timid in its policy research and advocacy roles, and the presidents collectively through the PC have not been as aggressive as many would like in defining a statewide vision for higher education.

Leadership, Vision, and Risk Taking Count

Leadership is critical to the process of deregulation. It is the governor and the legislative leaders who can change the laws to give deregulation a chance, but institutional leaders are the ones who will determine whether deregulation succeeds.

College presidents, supported by trustees, must show how excellence and access to affordable public higher education can be delivered with less government regulation. They must be able to overcome, at least some of the time, the parochial interests of their institutions in order to achieve a larger, collective good.

The New Jersey experiment rests on a basic precept of American higher education: local campus self-determination results in vision, quality, and direct accountability through trustee boards. Restructuring placed the burden for coordination on campus leaders, not on state bureaucracy. Innovation and accountability for mission and outcomes at the campus level would be emphasized. Responsibility for coordination and advocacy would fall to those who hold the colleges in public trust: boards of trustees and presidents. The great test of restructuring in New Jersey will be whether the campus leaders can achieve these lofty goals without direct state regulation.

Part Three

Making Deregulation Work

Chapter Six

State Policy for a Time of Adaptive Change

Patrick M. Callan
Kathy Reeves Bracco
Richard C. Richardson, Jr.

Twenty years ago, in the mid-1970s, the Carnegie Foundation for the Advancement of Teaching pointed out that the role of the states in higher education was growing more important. It saw little likelihood of new federal initiatives and noted that contemporary issues—the need for greater access and for more effective coordination—varied across the states. The report expressed confidence that states would find effective solutions, but it also expressed concerns over the tendencies in some states toward centralized government, overregulation, and parochialism—tendencies that "would reduce the adaptability to new circumstances and the chances for improvement" (Carnegie Foundation, 1976, p. 7).

In the mid–1990s, the nation's continuing need for dynamic colleges and universities is even greater than the authors of the Carnegie report could have envisioned. Developing talent and the nation's intellectual capital are increasingly recognized as crucial for national success in a global, information-based economy (Marshall and Tucker, 1992; Thurow, 1996; Drucker, 1993). Moreover, the role of the states has assumed even greater importance in an era of devolution and massive federal deficits.

Over the next decade, higher education will face a much different environment from that in which it has operated in the past. Five factors in this environment in particular will require difficult and perhaps traumatic response, and these are described in the first section of this chapter, since understanding and acceptance of reality is the first step in responding to it. The second section poses three challenges to states that arise from this new institutional environment and suggests the nature of the state and institutional leadership that will be needed to respond to it adequately.

A New Institutional Environment

The emerging institutional environment is formidable not because its elements are unfamiliar, but because they aggregate changes of a greater magnitude than any other since the period immediately following World War II. We believe that five elements are the most salient.

Increased Demand for Higher Education

The nation's high school graduating classes will increase dramatically over the next fifteen years. By the year 2009, the number of high school graduates is projected to increase by 32 percent over 1992. In the peak year of 2008, high school graduates will exceed the total for 1979, the peak year of baby boom high school graduates. In the spring of 2008, 3.3 million young Americans will graduate from high school, in contrast to 2.5 million in 1992.

There are significant regional and state variations within this broad national picture. Some states, among them Louisiana, Wyoming, North Dakota, and Maine, will see declines in high school graduations, while other states, such as Nevada, California, and Florida, will experience dramatic increases—of over 200 percent, over 50 percent, and over 70 percent, respectively. In addition, the next generations of high school graduates will reflect the demographic shifts that are occurring in America. Young Americans are more ethnically heterogeneous. This is particularly true in states that will experience the greatest growth in the numbers of high school graduates (WICHE, TIAA, College Board, 1993; and Breneman, Estrada, and Hayward, 1995).

The projected increase in high school graduates will bring greater demand for college opportunity than at any other time since the first tidal wave of baby boomers reached college age in the 1960s and 1970s. This next generation of young college-aged students, dubbed "Tidal Wave II" by Clark Kerr (1991, p. 260), will test the national commitment to educational opportunity, a public policy commitment that has been taken for granted in the United States for three decades. The states and the nation will revisit this question of educational opportunity at a time when the reconfiguration of the American economy has diminished prospects for a middle-class standard of living for those without at least some education or training beyond the secondary level.

Growing Public Concern About Educational Opportunity

In the 1990s, neither the economically vulnerable middle class nor those who have historically participated at low rates in higher education have showed any inclination to reduce educational opportunity. Public opinion research indicates that an overwhelming majority of Americans believe that qualified and motivated students should have educational opportunity regardless of personal or family wealth. However, the same survey data show growing worry about access and affordability; public resistance to tuition increases has begun to appear in opinion polls as many public colleges and universities raised tuition dramatically during the recession of the early 1990s to compensate for state budget cuts. Large numbers of poll respondents have reported willingness to entertain substantial overhaul of higher education if necessary to maintain educational opportunity (Immerwahr and Farkas, 1993; Jacobs, 1996).

The sharpest criticism of higher education now comes from those members of the public who are most knowledgeable about its workings. These elite critics, many of whom sit on higher education governing boards and send their children to the most prestigious universities, remain absolutely convinced of the value and importance of college opportunity. They tend, however, to believe that higher education is behind other sectors in controlling costs and improving quality. Many believe that colleges and universities must address the same reform and restructuring that characterize other sectors of the country, particularly the corporate sector. Further, they register a strong belief that these steps must precede the appropriation of new resources to higher education and that now is the time to revisit its most fundamental purposes. These groups have less sympathy than the public at large for the financial problems of higher education. They believe that the golden age of higher education finance is long past and that it is time for colleges and universities to face up to reality (Immerwahr, 1995; Wadsworth, 1995; Harvey and Immerwahr, 1995).

Severely Constrained Resources

There is little reason to be optimistic that the financial support for higher education can grow at the rates of prior decades. Efforts to reduce federal student financial aid drastically appear to have been blunted for the time being. Still, just to keep up with enrollment growth, financial aid programs will need to increase by about 20 percent over the next decade, and no one is predicting that outcome. With respect to the other major federal role, the support of university research, no less authoritative a body than the President's Council of Advisors on Science and Technology acknowledged in its 1992 report that it would not be reasonable to anticipate continued growth in the system of research-intensive universities (PCAST, 1992). At the state level, the early 1990s were financially traumatic. A recent report on state expenditures in the 1990s from the Center for the Study of the States identified the major shifts in state expenditures that occurred between 1990 and 1994 and pointed out that higher education spending, as a proportion of total spending, was increased in only seven states. Most states lost ground as total state resources for higher education fell from 14 percent to 12.5 percent of the total. Not surprisingly, many states substituted tuition for state support (Gold and Ritchie, 1995). Clark Kerr, in a recent edition of *The Uses of the University*, added a chapter entitled "A New Age? From Increasing Federal Riches to Increasing State Poverty" (Kerr, 1995).

Despite growing concerns about public confidence, the roots of higher education's financial difficulties are in the national economy and the financial constraints of the public sector, not in evidence that it has fallen into popular disfavor. Declining rates of economic productivity and slow national and state economic growth account for much of the resistance of government and private individuals to significant tuition increases and financial support. In the states, competition from elementary and secondary education, health and social services, entitlements, corrections, and pressures on governors and legislatures for tax relief have severely squeezed the discretionary revenues available for investment in higher education. A recent analysis of the California budget projected slow state revenue growth, increased numbers of young and old in the population, and an expanding corrections budget because of mandatory sentencing laws. Under the most pessimistic scenario of these projections, the state by the year 2005 would be left with only 9 percent of its budget available to allocate outside of health and welfare, corrections, and public schools. Robert H. Atwell, president of the American Council on Education, the nation's leading advocacy group for higher education, has warned that higher education should not expect to increase its current share of gross domestic product (2.8 percent) or its share of state or federal funding until some time beyond the year 2010 (Atwell, 1992; RAND, 1996).

Quality Issues

In the early 1990s a prestigious national panel on higher education, the Wingspread Group, found a substantial gap between needs of American society and what that society actually received from its institutions of higher education. The report charged that too many college graduates could not read or write very well, lacked the skills for success in the modern workplace, and generally suffered from shallow intellectual preparation (Wingspread Group, 1993).

A national survey of adult literacy, which examined document, prose, and quantitative literacy, found very few college graduates scoring in the highest ranges in any of these categories. An unexpectedly large number were in intermediate and lower skill levels when asked to read and interpret newspaper articles and bus schedules, and to solve problems requiring fairly basic computational skills (Barton and Lapointe, 1995). In addition, a 1992 transcript analysis by the Department of Education showed that more than a quarter of the students receiving bachelor's degrees lacked history

courses, almost a third lacked mathematics courses, and nearly
40 percent lacked English or American literature courses in their
college curriculum (Adelman, 1992, p. 19).

Challenges and Opportunities of Electronic Technology

Technology has already revolutionized research and has had major
impact on college and university administration. The questions are
whether and how technology can strengthen quality and access,
and can reduce cost to improve the productivity of higher education. It is probably fair to say that technology has had much less
influence on teaching and learning than on scholarly research and
on administration.

Few thoughtful observers have asserted that technology is a
panacea for all the challenges facing higher education. Outside
the academy—and, to a lesser extent, inside it—there is a growing
belief that technology has the potential to have a major influence
on the delivery of instruction. Properly and systematically applied,
it can be a major tool to make some learning more individualized
and more active. The academy, however, has been slow to explore
and capitalize on technology's potential, perhaps to its own ultimate disadvantage. A recent roundtable on the role of technology
in restructuring higher education warned the higher education
community of the dangers of educational obsolescence and competition. "Institutions that neglect technology will run the risk in
the future of being marginalized in favor of educational systems
that more effectively serve a generation of learners accustomed to
the benefits of ubiquitous computing and communications....Out-
siders will use information technology as a lever to pry open a market that heretofore has been the exclusive domain of colleges and
universities.... Ironically, the same faculty members who are fight-
ing against any substitution of information technology for their
labors may find themselves blindsided down the road by a much
greater force that simply eliminates their institution altogether"
(Technology and Restructuring Roundtable, 1995, p. 12).

Martin Trow (1993, p. 4) once characterized technology as the
"wild card" in the future of higher education. On one hand, it is
impossible to anticipate fully its long-term ramifications; on the
other hand, it seems equally implausible to believe that it is not a

major piece of the puzzle of what teaching and learning will look like in the future. For those who argue for higher education reform, technology represents an important though certainly not the exclusive avenue for leveraging needed reforms. It can be a means to making learning more individualized; better structured to respond to the heterogeneity of student preparation, goals, and learning styles; more productive; and more effective in terms of actual student learning (Johnstone, 1993; Barr and Tagg, 1995).

Although these five clusters of factors or conditions in the emerging institutional environment are not exhaustive, they seem the most significant. They will give rise to pressures that challenge higher education's basic modes of operation, including instruction and the assessment of its results. It is not our purpose to suggest a doom-and-gloom scenario. Higher education is a dynamic enterprise that has successfully responded to past societal needs, providing access to quality education and producing world-class research. There is no reason to believe it will not be as successful in the future as it has been in the past, but without new approaches to a new environment, the response may be traumatic at best and inadequate at the worst.

Challenge and Response

The new institutional environment will attenuate what Clark Kerr (1991) has characterized as "a state period in higher education" when federal initiatives are unlikely and "the major initiatives will come from state and private sources" (p. 264). Since Kerr made this observation, we have seen the ballooning of federal debt, growing public reaction against big government, and, most recently, an intense national debate over "devolution" of governmental responsibilities. For higher education, a period of state initiative represents a return to the historical norm, for states have always been the primary source of public policy guidance and support.

In contrast to most of its recent history, however, much of American higher education now faces conditions that cannot be effectively addressed within the repertoire of already known technical responses. Because in the aggregate the conditions confronting many colleges and universities and state systems of higher education pose fundamental challenges to values and behavior, they require another order of change. The emerging institutional environment poses three major challenges for higher education over the coming decades:

1. Maintaining and improving quality, efficiency, and access without significantly greater financial resources
2. Accommodating the new tidal wave of enrollments without commensurate increases in financial resources or staffing
3. Harnessing powerful electronic technologies to improve the accessibility, quality, and cost-effectiveness of instruction

Traditional State Approaches to Higher Education Policy Direction

Many traditional state approaches to higher education policy direction and guidance no longer seem viable in the new institutional environment. At the risk of oversimplification, many past approaches can be characterized as centralization-regulation or indifference-deference.

Centralization may have less to offer now than it did in the 1950s, 1960s, and 1970s. Richard Novak (1996) points out that most governance changes that occurred then "moved toward a consolidation of authority into the hands of fewer boards and higher level administrators" (p. 19). Many states have followed this centralization-regulation approach by increasing controls over higher education through statutes and budget control language.

Another approach—the one often preferred by higher education leaders—is for the state to "leave it to the experts." This is the approach of either indifference or deference to the wishes of the professional and institutional community. Despite the decades of increased regulation and control, higher education is still subject to less regulation than any other major state function ("Higher Education," 1995). This relative freedom from regulation is generally considered positive, but the strategy of indifference-deference can also reflect a low level of interest and priority on the part of state political leaders. In any case, the approach is at best a double-edged sword.

Neither of these two approaches is likely to address the new environment effectively. Although greater centralization may scratch an immediate gubernatorial or legislative itch, it most often adds to expense by increasing bureaucracy and transaction costs. More seriously, by limiting flexibility, it leaves institutions less able to respond to change. The indifference-deference approach, although it does not add costs or administrative complexity, has the disadvantage of depriving higher education of the policy stimulus it needs to respond to broader public interests. As Derek Bok, the former Harvard president, expressed in his book *Universities and the Future of America* (1990), "The fact remains that left entirely to their own devices, academic communities are no less prone than other professional organizations to slip unconsciously into complacent habits, inward looking at standards of quality, self-serving standards of behavior. To counter these tendencies, there will always be a need to engage the outside world in a lively continuing debate about the university's social responsibilities" (p. 111). In a world of political and public policy indifference, the tendency of colleges and universities to be inwardly focused is accentuated, and the danger becomes one of increasing irrelevance. The healthy tension between the academy and society—between the public interest as articulated by public officials and the institutional and professional interests of administrators and faculty—is a necessary tension that is lost in the indifference-deference mode.

The Federal Model: An Alternative Approach

A federalist model offers an alternative to the indifference-deference and centralization-regulation approaches. Federalism is typically thought of as applying to countries, but all organizations can be thought of in federal terms.

Handy (1994) says that a federal system seeks to be both centralized and decentralized, local in many of its decisions but global in its scope; federal systems have a strong center that is devoted to the service of its parts and seek to maximize independence while maintaining a necessary interdependence. A federal model is useful because it provides a structure of checks and balances for managing tensions that inevitably characterize institutional relationships with state authority, demographic pressures, and changing technology. Federalism deals with these tensions by providing stakeholders with opportunities to influence the decisions that affect their interests. Providing forums where students, employers, and other interested parties can participate in discussions about programs, services, and costs complicates the policy environment by eliminating the assumption that elected officials and ethical professionals adequately consider the public's interests in their decision-making processes. At the same time, federalism—so long as it does not evolve into centralization or devolve into deference—offers the promise of management autonomy within a context that promotes cooperation, economies of scale, and flexibility.

Because federal systems seek to balance conflicting interests, they typically satisfy no one. As a result, they are subject to frequent revisions by governors, legislators, or institutional constituencies who correctly perceive their special interests might be better served by the centralization-regulation or indifference-deference approaches. It is the constant pulling and tugging for more responsive structural arrangements by representatives of special interests that gives federalism its dynamic quality. It is this same struggle that creates fairly uniform dissatisfaction with the structures that are created to implement federalism. Their survival can be attributed more to the inability of stakeholders to reach consensus about the direction of desired changes than any endorsement of performance. Nobody loves a referee, but contestants need them. Similarly, federal models have all of the limitations and liabilities of a democracy; fortunately they also have many of the strengths.

Handy (1992, p. 67) provides five defining principles that are crucial for an effective federal model. The first, subsidiarity, aims at preserving the legitimate role of operating units by keeping the center small and avoiding centralized decisions that can be made at lower points. The second, interdependency, is achieved through the reserved powers of the center. The third principle, a common law, language, and currency, involves agreement on the basic rules of conduct and a common way of communicating. The fourth, twin citizenship, involves the degree to which participants in a system concurrently feel themselves a part of both the larger system and the operating unit to which they have their primary allegiance. The fifth principle, separation of powers, has to do with placing the management, monitoring, and governance functions of an organization in separate units.

All of Handy's principles are illustrated in the approaches that Illinois has brought to state governance (Richardson, 1996). The

Illinois State Legislature, which has not wanted the Illinois Board of Higher Education (IBHE) to be too strong, easily turned aside a 1995 effort to strengthen board powers despite the support of a strong governor. Whenever the board appears heavy-handed in its efforts to shape institutional decisions—as in its 1988 effort to strengthen admission requirements or in the more recent attempt to force institutions to merge or close programs—the legislature intervenes, or institutions successfully stonewall. The Illinois system clearly preserves the decision-making authority of individual institutions (subsidiarity), sometimes at the expense of faster progress toward articulated state priorities.

At the same time, the Illinois system gives evidence of substantial interdependence. The powers reserved to the IBHE in the budget, program review, and program approval processes prevent institutions from ignoring state concerns. Even private institutions respond to board initiatives as part of the price they pay to ensure that they are not unfairly undercut by the public sector.

Third, Handy's concept of common law, language, and currency can be found in the high-quality information provided to all stakeholders by the board, which provides a common way of communicating and a common unit of measurement. System participants also value the consensus-building approaches the board uses to create agreement on the basic rules of conduct. Policy officials and higher education professionals in Illinois argue that the system works not because these rules are written into statute but because they are not.

Handy's concept of twin citizenship may best be illustrated by the response to 1995 legislative action dismantling two system governing boards and replacing them with individual governing boards for eight of the nine affected institutions. At the time, the event was widely described by the media as "the end of the system of systems" and all that it had symbolized for Illinois higher education. As we write a year later, it is increasingly clear that although some of the rules of the game have changed and some constituencies have gained influence at the expense of others, the fundamental character of the system has been preserved and with it the continuing commitment of all stakeholders.

Finally, the Illinois system separates responsibility for management, monitoring, and governance. The decision to create individual governing boards for eight institutions during our study moved management closer to the presidential level in each of the affected institutions. IBHE monitors system performance through its highly sophisticated information system, as well as its key role in resource allocation, program review and approval, and articulation initiatives. Most leadership for significant change comes from the governor or his appointed representatives.

The Illinois decision to eliminate two system governing boards and replace them with individual boards may be seen as an effort to deregulate the system because it gives more power to the local institutions. However, Illinois continues to demonstrate characteristics of the federal model with some powers reserved to the center (governor, legislature, and IBHE) at the same time that significant decision-making powers are given to the institutional level. The elimination of the two system boards was an attempt to develop a better balance between the state and the individual institutions.

Illinois is by no means the only state system that operates according to identifiable federal principles. Texas uses a similar approach, although the system presents a different appearance because, unlike Illinois, the legislature, not the governor, has primary responsibility for providing state direction and leadership. McMahon (1996) describes the bill that restructured higher education in New Jersey by eliminating the Board and Department of Higher Education as intended "to create a balance between the flexibility that institutions need to carry out their individual missions and the statewide planning, coordination, and accountability required to meet the diverse needs of the state" (p. 7). This provides a clear example of federalism as a guiding principle.

Although we do not propose federalism as a panacea, we do believe it offers one productive alternative to the centralization-autonomy debate that has stifled productive discussions of state higher education governance for too long. To accommodate the multiple stakeholders in a democracy, we need alternatives to the Michigan model of deference-indifference, in which individual institutions yield no authority to the center, and the centralization-regulatory approaches of Georgia and Florida, which can subordinate institutional concerns to a central state bureaucracy. The fact that any model can work well given the right leadership and the right circumstances (Schick and others, 1992) suggests a need to extend our analysis by asking which of these approaches may be most and least susceptible to poor leadership or unusual circumstances.

Defining Conditions for Change

Throughout the post–World War II era, most enrollment and budgeting variations have been within fairly narrow ranges and were managed, although perhaps not always effectively, either by the institutions themselves or by central authority. Most institutions and states have the capabilities to address this normal give-and-take within existing systems as long as fundamental values and behavior remain unchallenged. The new environment now approaching seems likely, however, to require state government and state leaders to face challenges to their fundamental values. Adequate state response—response that stimulates and supports institutional adaptation—requires an understanding of the character of the changes facing colleges and universities. A framework for such understanding is suggested by Ronald A. Heifetz, who has related leadership strategies to the nature of the institutional and organizational changes required. Central to Heifetz's conception is the difference between technical and adaptive situations.

The conditions for technical change occur when both a problem and its solutions are clear and the solutions lie within the expertise and established repertoire of responses that institutions and organizations have developed. In other words, a problem exists, and the organization knows how to solve the problem using the previously learned behavior. The conditions for adaptive change, on the other hand, occur when neither the problem nor the solution is clearly defined. Both are outside the experience or competence of the organization.

For colleges, universities, and state systems of higher education, technical issues are those arising within the limits of the normal give-and-take of institutional and political life—for example, those arising in the normal variation in state budgets and enrollments or in the familiar requirements of program and enrollment allocation. Adaptive work is required in situations where institutional learning is needed to diminish the gap between the values people stand for and the realities they face—when addressing the problem "requires a change in values, beliefs, or behavior" (Heifetz, 1994, p. 22).

Except when institutional survival is at stake, pressure on public institutions for adaptive change almost always originates outside the academy. State officials are sometimes a source of such pressure as they reflect public concerns and identify and articulate gaps

between the outcomes produced by higher education systems—
often in terms of accessibility, quality, or cost—and public needs.
Absent some external statement of the problem, it is often difficult
for colleges and universities to raise the adaptive questions unilat-
erally. State leaders therefore can play a crucial role in initially
articulating the issues from the perspective of the broad public interest and engaging college and university leaders to address the
definitions and dimensions of the problem.

Defining the problem is critical, as Robert Reich (1988) has
written: "The act of raising the salient public question ... is often
the key step, because it subsumes the value judgments that declare
something to be a problem, focuses public attention on the issue,
and frames the ensuing public debate" (p. 5). At this point of problem definition, both political and educational leaders often first
succumb to what Heifetz (1994) has called "work avoidance mechanisms": "Finally, people fail to adapt because of the distress provoked by the problem and the changes it demands. They resist the
pain, anxiety, or conflict that accompanies a sustained interaction
with the situation. Holding onto past assumptions, blaming authority, scapegoating, externalizing the enemy, denying the problem,
jumping to conclusions, or finding a distracting issue may restore
stability and feel less stressful than facing and taking responsibility
for a complex challenge" (p. 37).

Definitions of both the problem and the required changes will
have to balance the broad public interest as articulated by the
states with the legitimate interests of the professional community.
Clearly, achieving such satisfaction will require social learning, the
reconciliation of competing values, and changes in attitudes and
behavior. Mutual satisfaction will not come easily. The tendency to
avoid engagement with a new reality is a characteristic of individuals, groups, and organizations throughout any process of adaptive change, but it usually first surfaces as a denial of the problem.
One form of denial is to assert that adaptive problems are cyclical
and therefore self-correcting or susceptible to technical solutions.
Some higher education leaders engaged in this behavior in the first
half of the 1990s, holding that an improved economy or a better
political climate would see a return to historical funding levels.
Political leaders are also susceptible to work-avoidance strategies.
One of the common ones is the raising of a "hot-button issue" that

diverts attention away from the adaptive challenge. Governor Pete Wilson of California, a state facing a dramatically increased enrollment demand of nearly half a million over the next decade, advocated eliminating affirmative action as the apparent cornerstone of his strategy to ensure educational opportunity. Whatever the merits of his argument against affirmative action, his position, knowingly or otherwise, distracted public and media attention from the fact that the state lacked any plan whatsoever for accommodating the projected enrollment growth.

Defining the adaptive challenge almost always requires public policy leadership. But resolution does not seem susceptible to either of the historical approaches states have usually taken. Neither the approach of indifference-deference nor that of centralization-regulation encourages the institutional learning that is needed and the changes in values, attitudes, and behavior required for adaptive change. Moreover, state strategies of indifference or excessive deference reinforce the inclinations of colleges and universities to avoid facing the need for change and to equate professional and institutional interests with an unarticulated public interest. Strategies of centralization and micromanagement tend to lock in outdated technical solutions when adaptive solutions are required, thereby impeding institutional learning and stimulating—even inspiring—resistance.

Strategic Assets for Addressing Adaptive Issues

Heifetz (1994, pp. 103–104) has identified the "strategic assets" (or structural characteristics) required for dealing with adaptive problems. These include a holding environment for containing stress, the capacity to command and direct attention, access to information, control over the flow of information, power to frame issues, the means to orchestrate conflict and contain disorder, and the power to choose decision-making processes. These assets are most evident in states that use federal principles and least apparent in the indifference-deference approach. For example, in Texas, a state that uses federal principles, the state Coordinating Board provides the holding environment for adaptive work because the board can command and direct attention to issues but cannot define problems or impose solutions absent institutional and legislative concurrence.

In Michigan, on the other hand, there is no holding structure; all issues are ultimately decided by individual institutions or by the legislature. In Florida, the Postsecondary Education Planning Commission lacks the authority and the inclination to serve in this role except as directed by the legislature on specific issues.

Access to information is another important strategic asset for addressing adaptive issues. Whereas both Florida and Texas have systems that provide reasonable access to timely and relevant information for all stakeholders, institutions in Michigan zealously guard data and have been successful in preventing the development of any information system other than the one used by the legislature to allocate appropriations.

Heifetz (1994) argues that "the leadership of adaptive work usually requires the orchestration of conflict" (p. 117). Even though our colleague Marvin Peterson argues with Michael McLendon in Chapter Eight of this book that informal mechanisms such as tradition and a council of presidents help to manage conflict in that state, our study of Michigan suggests that, apart from voluntary activity that promotes institutional interests, there is no mechanism in Michigan other than the governor and the legislature for orchestrating conflict and containing disorder, as evidenced by the 1995 budget process. Florida deals with conflict through bureaucratic authority, an approach that is not well suited to dealing with adaptive problems, as evidenced by the confrontations between the system chancellor and the president of the University of Florida over communication with legislators.

Our point is not to contrast these states in ways that praise or blame. Indeed, if we believed that the future will be an evolutionary extension of the past, we might well hold up Michigan as a shining example of every professional's prescription of how to create institutions that provide large measures of individual choice and program quality. Since we believe that the new environment will be qualitatively as well as quantitatively different in ways that cannot be fully predicted, however, we conclude instead that the Michigan model offers few strategic assets for adaptive work and that the Florida model offers more, but still fewer than states that make greater use of federal principles. To the extent that a state lacks the structural requirements for eliciting leadership from multiple sources that is designed into federalism, it must rely on individual institutional leaders (in the case of Michigan) or on system and institutional leadership (as in the cases of Georgia and Florida). To understand the implications of such reliance, we need to look more closely at the kinds of leadership that state systems are likely to require.

Stimulating Adaptive Change

Heifetz (1994) has identified five principles of leadership that might well serve as guidelines for state leaders in an era of adaptive change for higher education:

- *Define the adaptive challenge.* State leaders must take the initiative in identifying from the perspective of public interest the problems requiring adaptive change.
- *Regulate and manage the stress.* The external pressure to engage in adaptive behavior must be challenging but not overwhelming, and time must be allowed for the need to be understood. State incentives can strengthen the hand of institutional leaders in stimulating change.
- *Direct disciplined attention to the issue.* State leaders should keep colleges and universities to the fire and ensure that work avoidance does not impede progress. They should require information on progress and insist on accountability for results.
- *Give the work back to people.* The work of adaptive change of redesigning or reinventing programs and institutions must be the responsibility of the systems and institutions of higher education. Effective leadership strategies will keep a level of pressure on institutions without attempting to micromanage their processes or to take responsibility for the work away.
- *Protect threatened leadership voices.* It is important that the debate about higher education be a lively one, both within and outside colleges and universities. This is a time for more rather than fewer ideas. It will be important to listen carefully to the critics and those who say that responses go too far or not far enough. Efforts to exclude dissenting voices from the conversation are likely ultimately to be counterproductive.

We see Heifetz's principles as a useful lens for examining state capacities for change. Examples of the application of these principles can be seen in reform efforts currently under way in Virginia and Illinois. Although it is far too early for conclusive assessment, Virginia's restructuring effort, led by the State Council of Higher Education with legislative support, seeks to accommodate enrollment increases without additional per-student funding, improve the quality of undergraduate education, cut administrative overhead, and use computers and other educational technology. The program seeks to ensure that state policy objectives of access and quality are met. At the same time, it requires each institution to develop its own restructuring plan, and the plans and their implementation are monitored closely by the higher education council and the legislature. The council also has made it clear that its authority to make budget recommendations and to review new academic programs will be used to reward institutions that make progress (Trombley, 1995). Virginia, like Illinois, Texas, and New Jersey, makes extensive use of federal principles in the design of its higher education system. The legislature has resisted efforts by the governor to move away from such principles.

Illinois offers a second example, and one quite different from the Virginia approach. Its Priorities, Quality, Productivity (PQP) program was designed to reduce low-priority and duplicative academic programs, many at the doctoral level, and reallocate resources to undergraduate education and other priority areas. As in Virginia, the responsibility for making the decisions was left to the colleges and universities, with careful monitoring from the Board of Higher Education. This process had the strong support of the governor, who has made it clear that the PQP outcomes played a major role in his decision to increase funding for Illinois higher education (Trombley, 1996).

It is not yet certain that either the Virginia or the Illinois strategy will succeed in stimulating adaptive institutional change. The test will be whether colleges and universities ultimately respond by restructuring academic and administrative processes and programs in ways that improve efficiency, quality, and effectiveness. Yet both approaches are promising because the states and institutions are collaborating in developing new adaptive capacities.

These two examples do not begin to exhaust the range of strategies that states might employ. Reorganization of state higher education governance structures has been attempted by many states, with mixed results. Some reorganizations have improved higher education by effectively rebalancing the interests of the public, institutions, and students, sometimes a necessary condition for adaptive change. Other reorganizations have—usually unintended by policymakers—deflected attention from more fundamental substantive issues related to the performance of higher education and thereby caused work avoidance (Novak, 1996).

A more drastic state strategy, often advocated but attempted less frequently than organizational change, is the restructuring of public finance of higher education. One version is to condition major portions of state appropriations on institutional performance in areas determined to be high state priorities. Another is to devote most financial support of higher education to need-based student financial aid programs that put dollars directly into the hands of the consumers of higher education. Both of these public finance strategies would reduce state allocations for the maintenance and support of institutions and seek to stimulate institutional responses to state priorities or the student market. In the former version, state financing becomes a set of incentives for institutional performance; in the latter, incentives arise out of greater student purchasing power in a market characterized by intensified competition among public institutions and between public and private institutions.

These strategies are not mutually exclusive. In Illinois, a major governance restructuring occurred during the PQP process. At the same time, new financial incentives permitted colleges and universities to reinvest their PQP savings in areas of high institutional priority. Strategies will necessarily vary from state to state. There is no "one-size-fits-all" approach to adaptive change. Nevertheless, we suggest that the crucial initial steps are similar:

1. Identify the policy problem(s) from a public interest, as well as a professional and an institutional, point of view.
2. Establish challenging but manageable rates of change.
3. Include rigorous monitoring by and accountability to state leaders.
4. Provide institutional responsibility for designing and implementing the actual changes in academic programs.

In implementing these steps, states need to inventory their strategic assets for adaptive change and consider adopting federal principles where too much is left to the performance of one or a few

key leaders. As we were told by the chair of the Illinois Board of
Higher Education during one of our visits to that state, "Good leaders can overcome structural deficits, but they shouldn't have to."

Conclusion

Over the next two decades, state leaders will be called on to give
policy leadership and guidance to their institutions of higher education. A new institutional environment will pose new challenges,
and governors and legislatures must avoid easy reliance on past
approaches to leadership. They must identify the challenges in
terms of the public interest, allow time for institutions to face reality, yet ensure that change is taking place. For the most part, institutional changes should be designed by the institutions of higher
education themselves, and they must not turn deaf ears to dissenting voices. The challenge to state leaders is as great as that to
the colleges and universities; without effective state leadership,
there is less likelihood of institutional response that will strengthen
standards of access and quality.

Chapter Seven

Rethinking the Criteria for Trusteeship

Richard T. Ingram

Releasing public colleges and universities from excessive state regulation, if adroitly managed, will lead to better results for students, the institutions that serve them, and the public, which supports the enterprise. Critical to the success of the new autonomy are boards of trustees with the savvy and the authority to govern responsibly in the deregulated environment. Right now, this is not always the case. Too many partisan appointed or elected board members see colleges and universities as typical of state agencies that are theirs to exploit for political or personal purposes. And the most capable and well-meaning trustees find themselves deliberating endlessly over trivial bureaucratic issues because they often find that the real power lies elsewhere. To make difficult matters worse, scorching sunshine laws rule out serious, truly reflective, and controversial discussions in academic boardrooms in many states.

All of this ought to change if public colleges and universities, and the systems of these institutions, are to address the economic, political, and social challenges before them. The direction this change takes should be guided by two related trends. First, whether as result of a conscious policy decision or because of circumstance, public institutions are coming to look more and more like private ones every day. As state appropriations dwindle and public institutions come to rely more on tuition dollars and external support, the distinctions between public and private blur. This transformation in university financing calls for a change in the kinds of trustees who govern them and in the work those trustees perform.

Second, in addition to the substantive deregulation in New Jersey, which Darryl Greer describes in Chapter Five, there are less dramatic attempts in states across the country to shift to self- (as opposed to bureaucratic) regulation. Public universities and systems are seeking, and occasionally receiving, authority to manage their own legal affairs, build buildings and let bonds, and establish their own personnel policies without the approval of state agencies. These new responsibilities, which also illustrate a kind of privatizing, call for trustees with experience in making decisions with real consequence in complex organizations. Rising expectations and political clout of interest groups along with a decline in support to meet those expectations have made it more difficult to manage public institutions. In this highly constrained environment, trustees, along with their presidents and chancellors, need to be granted more freedom of action to find the best solutions among too few good options.

This chapter proposes new models of public trusteeship and governance of tax-supported colleges and universities. The ideas here are hybrid, borrowing from the best practices of private and public boards. They will require considerable support and not a little courage from state government if they are to be implemented successfully. Although its context is the four-year institution, the proposal is relevant to the governance of public two-year community colleges as well.

The Case for Reform

The governance of public colleges and universities, including the operations of their governing boards, should be reformed. Part of the reason is very simple: there are too few governing board members on the public side to do the work. In addition, the dynamic economic, political, social, and demographic circumstances demand a new style of board leadership.

Never Have So Many Been Governed by So Few

In the academic year 1995–1996, the University of Michigan, with three campuses, had revenue from all sources totaling $2.57 billion, 28,648 employees, and a total enrollment of 51,000. Its governing board has only nine regents, elected statewide through a political party nomination process. In the same year, the State University of New York, with sixty-four campuses, had total revenues of $5.39 billion, 72,219 employees, and a total enrollment of 381,000 students. Its governing board of sixteen trustees, including one student trustee, is appointed by the governor and ratified by the state Senate. The Los Angeles Community College District, with nine campuses, had annual revenues of $377 million, 5,713 employees, and a total enrollment of 98,000 students. Its governing board of only seven trustees, including a student, is elected district-wide. And the fifteen campuses of the University of Texas had an aggregate annual budget of $4.2 billion, 68,956 employees, and a total enrollment of almost 150,000. Its governing board of nine members is appointed by the governor and ratified by the Senate.

Nationwide, the American people and their elected representatives entrust more than sixteen hundred public four- and two-year colleges and universities with a total full- and part-time enrollment of 11.7 million students and revenue from all sources, in 1993, totaling $120 billion, to the oversight of only ten thousand appointed and elected trustees and regents. (Of the $120 billion, about one-third, or $40 billion, were state funds.) The average public institution or system board ranges from five to thirty members. The public community college board typically has seven or nine members; the four-year institution or system board more like fifteen members. By way of contrast, private higher education, with less than three million students, is governed by approximately forty thousand trustees. The imbalance of trustee-student ratios between the public and private sectors is due to the existence of so many multicampus system boards in public higher education, coupled with their average size of only fifteen members.

The current configuration of governing boards of public colleges and universities and how their members are selected borders on irrational, especially given the new environments and realities confronting public higher education. By what logic can we vest such enormous responsibilities to oversee such enormous enterprises in so few trustees and regents?

The Economic Situation Is Changing

In the face of other pressing priorities and mandated requirements, state appropriations for higher education have become a major source of discretionary spending available to governors and legislators. In state after state, higher education outlays are the first to be cut from the budget and the last to be restored. Tuitions at public colleges and universities have risen significantly in percentage terms as state support has declined, especially since 1990, and the high tuition–high aid model is likely to be debated as never before, as will the case for differential tuitions by institutional mission and degree program. In effect, falling state support and rising fees combine to privatize public higher education whether or not legislators make a conscious policy decision to do so.

There is increasing doubt that parents of eighteen- to twenty-five-year-old students with above-median family incomes should pay the same heavily subsidized prices as those whose current income is well below average. In state after state, the leaders of public colleges and universities have been unable to do realistic multiyear budget or capital planning. The first five years of the 1990s were replete with major annual cuts in state appropriations, followed by surprise midyear cuts to help balance state budgets. It has not been a pretty picture, and no one confidently predicts a return to yesteryear.

The good old days of collegiate financing included a combination of state appropriations, tuition, and capital funding requests. Funding for public higher education now involves less, and less predictable, state funding, significantly higher tuition, complex subsidiaries and auxiliary operations including hospitals, and much more reliance on private philanthropy and the work of campus foundations. Again, the distinctions between public and private institutions diminish as the need for external, nonstate sources of revenue grow. This change in funding calls for additional public trustees who have the influence, the capacity, the inclination, and often the personal capacity to find private money.

The point is that the economics of higher education and the economic relationship between state government and public higher education have changed and continue to do so significantly. The debate about whether public higher education is primarily a public good or an individual benefit, and who should pay for it, is on again. State dollars as a significant portion of total revenue—generally available until recently—have declined; paradoxically, demands of political leaders for more productivity and greater accountability have brought more regulation, not less. Under the convenient label of accountability, we find many state governments and their education bureaucracies dangerously and inappropriately imposing a cookie-cutter approach to performance assessment, one first imposed on public K–12 education, where standardized tests and multiple-choice questions are the norm.

The role of public college and university foundations to raise and manage private dollars from individuals, corporations, and foundations has taken on unprecedented importance in the financing of public colleges and universities. As their carefully selected members continue to be strengthened with influential alumni and alumnae and others committed to institution building and philanthropy, and as public college and university leaders use the technology of fundraising to its fullest advantage, it is becoming increasingly likely that the truly exceptional public institution will be one that has an exceptional foundation.

These Challenges Require More from Trustees

These changes bear on trustees and governing boards and the need for reform in several important ways. Governing boards must be large enough and include people with the commitment, philanthropic spirit, broad-based knowledge of big budgets, and complex organizations to cope successfully with these new economic realities. They must be credible leaders in their respective fields in order to hold the respect of the members of their institution's foundation and state's political leaders, as well as to advocate effectively for their institutions and help them to adjust to market forces. Only men and women of substantial accomplishment and experience will be able to set tuition policies intelligently to compete, serve as personal and collective examples of private philanthropy for others, and argue successfully with state political leaders that the state does indeed have a moral and legal responsibility to provide high-quality, adequately financed public colleges and universities. Too few people of this stature sit on public governing boards.

Politics May Favor These New Roles

There is an unmistakable shift in the mood of the nation toward reducing the size and intrusion of government, decentralizing decision making, revitalizing the entrepreneurial spirit of both individuals and institutions, restoring the influence of market forces, and reducing taxes. A timely survey of fifty-eight state House and

Senate education committee chairs in forty-nine states makes this conclusion: many legislators hope to create new decentralized systems that will be less bureaucratic and less political. They believe this can be achieved in part by consolidating some coordinating functions, appointing rather than electing regents, and eliminating multiple layers of decision making. Legislators also hope that by reallocating responsibilities, greater operational efficiency and academic effectiveness can be achieved (Ruppert, 1996, p. 21). Whether this ideology prevails in the long term remains to be seen, of course, but it does represent the belief that higher education should operate in a more competitive market environment with fewer regulatory constraints. Logically, this kind of thinking should also endorse the new roles for trustees described here.

Many Policymakers Oppose Deregulation

If many policymakers favor deregulation as a path to better performance, others prefer the heavy hand of central control as the way to get work done. A surprising number of newly elected governors and legislators seem to be unhappy with the performance of public institutions and their governing boards. They view them as the captives of their presidents and faculties, too soft on the hard issues such as academic and admission standards (especially undergraduate education), faculty teaching workloads and productivity, reallocation of resources, time-to-degree trends, campus crime rates, attrition rates, and on and on. Indeed, frustrated governors here and there are substituting their judgments for those of governing boards and their chief executives through increased regulation, line-item budgeting, and other performance-based requirements attached to appropriations bills.

There is widespread misunderstanding on the part of lawmakers about the responsibilities of trustees and governing boards of public higher education. One governor told me that, in his view, a good trustee is one who responds to the governor's concerns and advice. Another governor recently told an audience of new trustees, all of whom he appointed, that they should disabuse themselves of any notion that they should lobby for their institutions. Although there are exceptions, elected political leaders seem by and large to be unaware of why, in every state, public colleges and universities and systems of academic institutions have governing boards and what broad public interest and institutional purposes and functions they are there to serve.

There is criticism of trustee and governing board performance within the academy as well. It is not uncommon for presidents and chancellors, in moments of candor, to describe the behavior of some of their trustees as their biggest problem and their institution's biggest handicap. They cite examples where, in apparent efforts to prove that they are not rubber stamps for their administrators, trustees are increasingly micromanaging. They see trustees using their trusteeships to get their names in the newspaper or advance their own political ambition. They see trustees who do not do their homework but who are quick to demand reports, data, and information that they do not put to any good use.

It is nothing new for academic chief executives to report that partisan politics are rampant in boardrooms, that some state governors decide who should chair the board of the flagship university, that factions within boards often follow political party affiliation, that more trustees seem to be oriented to their own advancement and visibility than to public service and commitment to higher education, and that, overall, the stature and reputation of their trustees has generally declined. It is not uncommon for presidents and chancellors to report that the membership of their foundation(s) is much stronger, more consequential to their institution's progress than is the membership of their governing board.

Many of our most able citizens by virtue of their experience, skills, personal philanthropy, and deep commitment to higher education reject public trusteeship because they refuse to be part of boards that are politicized and function in all ways and at all times in the public fishbowl and operate under the heavy regulatory hand of state bureaucracies.

If citizen governing boards will prevail as a distinctive characteristic of higher education in the nation, as the only viable alternative to direct control by state government, which is prevalent in most other countries, they need to be enabled to do their jobs. The most attractive trustees—intelligent people with strong, independent views on the role of the university—are not going to accept appointments from governors who expect them to rubber-stamp their political initiatives.

Changing Social and Demographic Realities

The public university is difficult to lead and manage, especially as compared with the independent college or university, for several reasons. Their sheer size, complexity, and multiplicities of mission and purpose are surely part of the answer, as is their vulnerability to political pressure from special interest groups and politicians. The changing and challenging social context within which public universities function is also a major factor.

The proliferation of special interest groups, especially since the 1960s, and the fact that so many now make claim on the public university, causes it to be the lightning rod for nearly every ideology or cause from newly militant rightist groups to the furthest on the left. The principle of institutional neutrality on social and moral issues of the day is increasingly difficult to sustain. Public demands for access at affordable prices, even in the face of stable or reduced state appropriations, and persistent calls for cost containment bring tough choices into boardrooms; the ethnic and racial diversity of the student body occasions tensions on campuses because colleges and universities are on the front line of teaching people how to live with one another. The compelling issues of social justice and the underrepresentation of growing minority populations in student bodies, faculties, and college administrations, along with group politics that balkanize the campus, are among our preoccupations. More than ever, this clash of values requires sophisticated, diverse, aware, courageous, and committed trustees—in sufficient numbers—who can work effectively with their chief executive to do the right thing, to be fair to everyone without giving away the store or abdicating their responsibility to lead.

Demographers tell us that by the year 2010, there will 3.8 million fewer white children and an increase of 4.4 million nonwhite children, a majority of them from disadvantaged backgrounds, and with challenging issues of social policy confronting government and public higher education (Hodgkinson, 1993, pp. 33–34). It is largely the job of the public, not the private, institutions to educate these new learners. Our multicultural campuses have experienced some tension here and there, but there are more turbulent times ahead. Unless state legislators and governors are prepared to become the front line of decision makers on how campuses should respond to these dramatic social and demographic changes, they should be assuring themselves that boards of public higher education are positioned to do so.

The Renewed Governing Board

Given the enormity of the changing economic, political, and social environments, how is the public college or university best governed and led? What principles should guide the size, composition, selection, and responsibilities of the board of trustees? To inform and guide reform, which institutions currently embody one or more of these principles in their policies and practices?

For the uniquely American institution of citizen trusteeship to function effectively in contemporary higher education, state statutes and regulations should enable the governing boards of public colleges and universities to have members with the following characteristics:

- Recruited to their responsibilities from and by multiple sources, who meet explicit qualifications and have significant records of personal achievement and broad experience— especially with large, complex organizations and budgets.
- In sufficient numbers to share the required workload through a sensible committee structure appropriate to the institution and the board's broad range of responsibilities. (There is much to be said for a governing board that can conduct most of its work through an effective committee structure rather than as a committee of the whole, with committees having only two or three members, or with a structure where trustees must serve on more than two committees because of their small number.)
- Positioned to help the institution to raise significant dollars from private sources—men and women who are themselves willing and able to practice the spirit of philanthropy, by personal and collective example, consistent with their means.
- Drawn from the ranks of alumni and alumnae, diverse in their ethnic, racial, and gender makeup.
- Selected as at-large state residents, without any requirement of geographical representation, such as by voting district or county.

- With terms long enough to ensure leadership continuity, knowledge of the institution, and deep commitment to its development.

   In addition to their traditional responsibilities and authority for stewardship and policy setting, these board members should hold the specific power to do the following:

- Set tuition levels, without political interference, and set the amount of institutionally funded student financial aid
- Allocate monies between and among budget lines without prior state approval
- Manage and invest all institutional funds, including private contributions, which they should be expected to help raise
- Determine their personnel policies and practices independent of the state's personnel system
- Determine the most efficient procurement policies and practices
- Otherwise manage the institution's internal affairs, without interference from the executive or legislative branches

Trustee Selection

The Association of Governing Boards of Universities and Colleges (AGB) has advocated the reform of trustee selection processes since an independent commission, chaired by former governor Bob Scott of North Carolina, published its report, *Recommendations for Improving Trustee Selection in Public Colleges and Universities* (1980). Jean Graves McDonald's *Changing State Policies to Strengthen Public University and College Trustee Selection and Education* (1995) assesses selection processes in Minnesota, Massachusetts, and Kentucky, and the reactions to legislation that mandates statewide trustee and education programs in Oklahoma and Kentucky. These two reports make the case for independent screening mechanisms of committed citizens who can help to depoliticize the process of gubernatorial appointment, discourage any notion that boards of trustees should act like minilegislative bodies, and encourage the notion that governing boards should see themselves and be seen by others as nonpartisan, deliberative bodies that serve the broad public interest and institutional advocacy.

More recently, an independent commission chaired by former Virginia governor Gerald L. Baliles, urges governance reforms. In *Renewing the Academic Presidency: Stronger Leadership for Tougher Times* (1996), the distinguished Commission on the Academic Presidency offers recommendations to presidents, boards, faculty, and public officials. Among its recommendations to state political leaders is an urgent call for

- Adoption of explicit, public statements of the qualifications to be sought for trustees of public colleges and universities
- Creation of independent panels of citizens to advise governors and legislators on trustee nominations that employ merit criteria
- Enlarged governing boards (at least fifteen members) selected from diverse sources of appointees, in consultation with board chairs and presidents who are in the best position to advise on needed skills, experience, and talent
- Greater independence from regulation in exchange for demonstrated results
- Redefinition of "sunshine" requirements, especially as they relate to presidential searches

Exemplary Practices

The principle of recruiting prospective trustees from and by multiple sources is particularly noteworthy. It has been practiced for many years with great success at a number of public universities, including the Pennsylvania State University, Cornell University, the University of Delaware, and Delaware State University, among several others.

Pennsylvania State University

At Penn State, a university whose governing board has a national reputation for effective leadership, the thirty-two-member board consists of six trustees appointed by the governor, nine elected by the

alumni through the General Alumni Association, six elected by organized agricultural societies, six elected by organized industrial societies, and five ex officio, including the president of the university,
the governor, and the secretaries of the state departments of agriculture, education, and conservation/natural resources. Penn State's
trustees are not bound by any residency requirement. Although they
come to their volunteer calling from multiple sources of appointment, the trustees do not see themselves as representing, individually or collectively, any special loyalty to them; their loyalties are in
serving their public trust and their university as a whole, not special
interest groups or political ideologies. The trustees have renewable
three-year terms (without limit), and many trustees have long and
distinguished records of commitment to personal philanthropy and
fundraising.

Cornell University

Private and public in its mission and funding, Cornell also has an
atypically large board, forty-two voting members, as follows: twenty-
one trustees at large elected by the board itself for staggered four-
year terms; eight elected from among and by the alumni for four-year
terms, without requiring state residency; four ex-officio trustees (the
governor, president of the state Senate and speaker of the assembly,
and the president of the university), three trustees appointed by the
governor with Senate confirmation for staggered three-year terms;
two faculty trustees for four-year terms; two student trustees for two-
year terms; one nonacademic staff/employee for a four-year term;
and one life trustee—the eldest lineal descendant of Ezra Cornell.
The university recently created a category of nonvoting trustee fel-
lows to work with the voting trustees in fostering relationships with
alumni and friends originally as part of a recent major capital campaign; they may not be board officers but are encouraged to participate in all board meetings and may chair board committees. Except
for the alumni trustee category, all trustees otherwise eligible and
under the age of seventy-three may be reelected or reappointed without limitation. This is a complex arrangement, to be sure, but Cornell also has a national reputation for consistent board leadership
and commitment to advancing the university.

St. Mary's College of Maryland

A public liberal arts honors college, St. Mary's presents a particularly interesting case. Its former president described its 1992 agreements with the state legislature and governor as providing it with more autonomy than any other public college or university in the country (Lewis, Muller, and Aery, 1994). The quid pro quo is described in more detail by Robert Berdahl in Chapter Four, but the essential element of agreement with the state concerns future appropriations to the college: by law, it now receives a general fund appropriation that is equal to the prior year, augmented by an inflationary adjustment based on the implicit price deflator for state and local governments index. Thus, the state will fund a smaller percentage of the college's total operating budget in the future. State funding is projected to decrease from about 50 percent of the college's total budget to 40 percent in fiscal year 1997 (and less in succeeding years).

Although the governor retains the authority to appoint its seventeen trustees (eventually to be twenty-five members), he is committed to appointing those persons nominated by the board of trustees (subject to legislative confirmation). Thus, the St. Mary's governing board, in accepting significant additional responsibilities in fundraising and policy determination in return for significant new freedom from government bureaucracy and political interference, is given the responsibility of carefully selecting candidates who will accept the new expectations and obligations it has accepted for itself.

St. Mary's is a noteworthy experiment that state government leaders could model with at least one or two public institutions whose leaders are willing to strike the same understandings. But the essential point is that highly qualified citizens are willing to be recruited to public boards and to accept fund giving, fundraising, and many other expanded responsibilities (as their counterparts in independent higher education readily accept), in return for having themselves and their institutions released from the constraints of state regulation—and provided they have a voice in determining who will fill vacancies on the board.

A report by a special board committee of the St. Mary's board of trustees, whose charge was to help the board prepare for expanded responsibilities brought on by the new relationship with the State of Maryland, describes the college's transition from being a totally public institution to one that has characteristics of both a public and a private institution. Chaired by Steven Muller, former president of Johns Hopkins University, the committee made this observation:

> In effect, the Trustees will need to become both leaders and managers in the best sense. In order to accomplish this they will need, at all times, to be attuned to a highly refined, clearly articulated vision of the College that is both near and long-term. They will need to be thoroughly knowledgeable about the College's fiscal, academic, and administrative operations. They will need to serve as consensus builders among all parts of the College community. Above all, they will need to become powerful advocates among individuals, corporations, and foundations, for gifts and grants to St. Mary's College. In short, they will need to lead the College vigorously in ways that have not been required of them before. [St. Mary's College of Maryland, 1992, p. 2]

In recognizing the importance of recruiting new board members who could fulfill these expectations, the committee concluded that future trustees should be found from among those who had proved their commitment to and involvement with the college:

> Strategies need to be developed to identify such individuals—individuals who will meet one or more of the following criteria: alumni; parents of current students or alumni; individuals representing the more populated counties of Maryland…; recognized corporate or business leaders in Maryland and Washington, D.C.; leaders in the Southern Maryland community; individuals of substantial financial means and/or access to individuals or businesses of substantial financial means; and greater representation of women and minorities. [St. Mary's College of Maryland, 1992, p. 3]

University of Virginia

The University of Virginia's board of visitors is also worthy of mention. Its sixteen-member governing board is appointed by the governor with Senate confirmation, but up to three trustees may be appointed from among alumni or alumnae living outside Virginia;

with regard to Virginia residency, there is no other requirement. It is especially interesting that at least eleven of the sixteen board members must be graduates of the university. Furthermore, the Alumni Association is invited to propose three names to the governor for each vacancy; although the governor is not obligated to accept this advice, many governors over the years have chosen to do so. The trustees have four-year terms, renewable once.

Other Universities

With a board of thirty-two voting members, including the governor of the state, the president of the university, the master of the state grange, and the president of the state board of education as ex officio members, the University of Delaware has a substantive board. Of the other twenty-eight trustees, eight are appointed by the governor, and twenty are elected by a majority of the board of trustees; both the governor's and the board's choices must be confirmed by the state Senate, and all are limited to a maximum term of six years.

Delaware State University has an eleven-member board; six trustees are appointed by the governor, and five are elected by a majority of the trustees themselves. All have six-year, renewable terms, without limit. In Pennsylvania, the University of Pittsburgh, Lincoln University, and Temple University, as state-related universities, have a mix of trustees selected by the governor and their own governing boards.

Enabling Governing Boards

State lawmakers have three basic choices as they shift their attention from K–12 reform and their many other important preoccupations, including health care, to higher education and its governance: maintain the status quo, increase bureaucratic and statutory regulations, or restore much more autonomy to their public colleges and universities. In states where the third course is taken, I argue for strengthening the capacity of public governing boards and trustees (and, implicitly, their chief executives) to do their jobs.

Transforming public trusteeship means closing the gap between the expectations for governing boards and the authority and freedom of action they in fact possess. This gap varies from state to state, and even from institution to institution within a given state, but it seldom diminishes.

A Checklist for Effective Trusteeship

Answers to the following questions may help policymakers to decide whether the governance of public college and university trusteeship in their state needs an overhaul:

1. Do elected officials understand the responsibilities of governing boards—what they should and should not be expected to do? Is there a clear job description for each governing board that addresses the rationale for their independence from state government and the balance they should maintain in serving the public trust *and* institutional advocacy?
2. Do the system or institutional governing boards have clear job descriptions for individual board members—what they are expected to do, and not to do? Are trustees given such information before they accept appointment?
3. Are trustees and regents selected with care and without unreasonable reliance on political party affiliation or strictly political influence or favoritism or strict residency requirements? Is the board large enough and broad enough in its aggregate skills, knowledge, and influence to do its job well? Does a list of the desirable qualifications to be sought in qualified citizens for academic trusteeship exist, and is it adhered to?
4. Are governing boards given the independence and authority they need, with their presidents and chancellors, to exercise leadership for which they truly can and should be held accountable? Are they seen by lawmakers more as instrumentalities or extensions of state government, rather than as independent bodies with the clear mandate to serve the broad public interest as well as to be entrepreneurial and responsible advocates for their institutions?
5. Is the state open-meeting law unnecessarily restrictive to the point that it discourages rather than promotes good board leadership? For example, are board committee meetings ex-

empt to enable their members to be totally honest, candid, and truly reflective on complex issues confronting their institutions as they consider options to recommend to the board for further (and open) discussion and action? Can the board and its search committee ensure candidates for the presidency or chancellorship that their names will be held in strict confidence until it is clear that they are among the finalists? Can the board conduct periodic retreats and workshops to explore complex issues and opportunities, including self-evaluation of their performance, without being subject to sunshine legislation—provided they do not make any decision binding on their institution?

Next Steps

The first step to reform, and perhaps the easiest to initiate in most states, is probably to experiment. Every state has at least one, two, or three colleges or universities whose trustee and academic leaders are willing and able to work with the governor and legislature to transform their boards and working relationship with the state along the lines suggested in this chapter and elsewhere in this book. St. Mary's College of Maryland took such an initiative and is well on its way to demonstrating what it can do with its new freedoms and responsibilities. Coastal Carolina University in South Carolina is another example. Indeed, the best of the good policies and practices concerning governing board composition and selection outlined in this chapter have been in place in several leading institutions and provide a road map for reform on an experimental basis.

The second, and probably more important, step is to reconfirm the serious role of lay trustees as governors of these public institutions, then examine and reform the way they are selected, educated about their responsibilities, and empowered to govern. This chapter lays out promising policies and practices for increasing trustee responsibility and authority. This call for reform should be implemented and tested on a broad scale, but change will require extraordinary leadership from extraordinary and courageous political and business leaders—and from trustees themselves.

Our dependence on private citizens as volunteers to govern the great public institutions, as opposed to oversight by professional bureaucrats, is part of the genius of higher education in the United States. It predates the current interest in privatization by well over a century. In many states, financial pressures coalesce with deliberate public policy choices to deregulate higher education and, perhaps, make it more competitive. States that systematically rethink and reform patterns of trustee leadership will be well positioned to take advantage of this new freedom.

Chapter Eight

Achieving Independence Through Conflict and Compromise: Michigan

Marvin W. Peterson
Michael K. McLendon

The process of state-level regulation or coordination and control of higher and postsecondary education has been constantly changing since the end of World War II. Although many and varied governing and coordinating structures have emerged in the fifty states, the pattern of the past four decades in virtually all of them has been one of increasing centralization of control and erosion of institutional autonomy, whether it was accomplished by the reorganization of state coordinating and governing structures, the action of executive agencies or legislative bodies in mandating greater coordination and control, or the accretion of staff and procedural controls by existing state higher education agencies. However, the recent trend toward deregulation that began at the federal level has been transmitted to the level of state government and is now emerging in our patterns of statewide governance and coordination of higher education, potentially reversing the four-decade-old trend.

This potential reversal resurrects the inverse of an intense debate of the 1960s and early 1970s: Rather than asking: "What is the impact of increased state-level regulation of higher education?" the questions become: "What is the impact of decreasing state regulation?"

and "How does the degree of state-level decentralization and reducing coordination and control (increasing institutional autonomy) affect the quality and performance of a state's higher and postsecondary system?" Although four decades of research on this topic have provided no clear answers (Hearn and Griswold, 1994) to this debate, and it is beyond the scope of this chapter to resolve it, it is instructive to examine the history, performance, and dynamics of one state with a well-regarded higher education system that has maintained a strong pattern of state deregulation and institutional autonomy: Michigan.

Postsecondary Education in Michigan

The establishment of a comprehensive, high-quality, and quite autonomous system of higher and postsecondary education in Michigan is largely a process of historic evolution in which the character of the state and its system of higher education have been shaped by many forces. In fact, the University of Michigan, chartered in 1817 by the Territory of Michigan as a classical and common school responsible for all public education, actually preceded Michigan's formal admission to the union as a state in 1837. Three public institutions founded between 1849 and 1885 addressed varying needs of the emerging state. The Agriculture College of the State of Michigan (1855) became the nation's pioneer land-grant institution, Michigan State University; a normal school (1849) became Eastern Michigan University; and the Michigan Mining School (1885) became Michigan Technological University. By 1903, as the state's population grew, three additional normal schools were added and later became Central, Western, and Northern Michigan universities. Lacking an urban institution to serve its needs, Detroit founded the College of the City of Detroit (1933), which later became a state institution, Wayne State University.

In the post–World War II era of economic prosperity, population growth, and national commitment to higher education, five more public institutions were added to serve growing regions of the state: Lake Superior State (1946, a former Michigan Technological University branch) in the upper peninsula and Ferris State (1950, a former private institution), Grand Valley State University (1960), Saginaw Valley State University (1963), and Oakland University

(1957, a former Michigan State University branch) in the lower peninsula. Between the end of World War II and 1968, twenty-three of the state's twenty-nine community colleges were founded.

This expansion of public higher education occurred without a statewide master plan or a state government agency planning higher education for the state. Institutions emerged as state needs received legislative priority, as local communities developed their own institutions, as existing institutions developed branches, or as legislators pressed for institutions in major unserved locations. An expanding population, a thriving economy, a strong public commitment to education, and local initiative created a public system by 1963 that largely reflects the system today.

Diversity and Comprehensiveness

Today Michigan, a large state with a complex economy, has a comprehensive system of postsecondary education institutions whose diversity of institutions, enrollment, and breadth of programs rivals that of most other large states. The public sector includes three Research I universities—the University of Michigan, a world-renowned research university; Michigan State University (MSU), a major land-grant institution; and Wayne State University, a premier urban university—which enroll over 125,000 students. A Research I university gives high priority to research, awarding fifty or more doctoral degrees per year and receiving $40 million or more annually in federal research support. The state's ten master's and doctoral universities serve approximately 140,000 students. Central, Eastern, Western, and Northern Michigan universities all offer a broad array of offerings at the undergraduate and graduate levels. Each of the remaining six institutions has a different focus. Michigan Technological University has expanded beyond its mining school history to build a technology focus. Ferris State has a special role in professional and applied education. Grand Valley, although now more traditional, began with an innovative undergraduate focus. Oakland University, originally a branch of MSU offering quality liberal arts, has expanded to serve the urban and suburban region north of Detroit. Lake Superior State and Saginaw Valley State reflect the particular needs of their regions of the state. The twenty-nine public community colleges, which serve around 220,000 students, are oriented to their own communities and financed by a combination of local support, state appropriation, and tuition and fees.

Although the public sector in Michigan enrolls considerably more students than the private sector, the latter is a significant part of the postsecondary system. There are fifty-nine private institutions enrolling over eighty-five thousand students. Although not represented by a research or doctoral university, this sector includes a major urban institution, the University of Detroit; strong liberal arts institutions like Albion and Kalamazoo; fiercely independent institutions like Hillsdale and Hope, which refuse federal aid; and many institutions with a special mission focus or clientele. One indication of the importance of these institutions for the state is the existence of three state-funded degree-reimbursement programs that provide direct institutional grants to private colleges and universities on the basis of the number of bachelor's, master's, and health-related degrees awarded annually (Yniguez, 1995). The proprietary sector is also a significant feature in Michigan. Approximately 229 institutions offer a highly varied array of specialized, professional, technical, and career-oriented programs, which enroll forty thousand students.

Thus, Michigan has a comprehensive system of higher education with a dominant public system but a significant private and proprietary presence. Education from the associate's degree through the doctorate is represented in varied fields. Within each sector, institutions have a diverse and often unique mission or clientele. It is a system in which there is considerable competition for students.

System Quality Indicators

The public postsecondary sector in Michigan is often viewed as among the best in the nation on several indicators of system quality. First, it is a geographically dispersed and accessible system of public institutions. The three research-doctoral institutions are located in the state's most populated southeast quadrant. The remaining ten comprehensive and regional universities are geographically dispersed across the more populous lower peninsula of the state (seven institutions) and the more rural upper peninsula (three institutions). The twenty-nine community colleges are similarly spread throughout the state. The major urban areas—Detroit, Flint/Saginaw, Lansing, and Grand Rapids—are all served by one of the three research universities or a branch campus, by one or more of the public comprehensive institutions, and by one or more local community college districts. Approximately 91 percent of all first-year students attending public colleges and universities in Michigan graduate from a Michigan high school, which is one of the highest rates in the nation (U.S. Department of Education, 1995).

Although the academic quality of a public system is hard to define, Michigan's institutions are regularly reputed to be among the best. Both MSU and the University of Michigan are members of the prestigious Association of American Universities, and the University of Michigan regularly ranks among the top two or three public universities in the nation on surveys of the quality of graduate education.

State financial support for public higher education in Michigan has declined over the past decade. Between fiscal year (FY) 1977 and FY 1986, the average annual percentage increase in state appropriations for higher education was 7 percent, but over the past ten-year period, from FY 1987 through FY 1996, the average annual percentage increase amounted to about half that—approximately 3.8 percent (Hines, 1996a, 1996b). Despite this decline, state financial support for public higher education in Michigan remains relatively strong. In FY 1996, for example, Michigan appropriated over $1.6 billion for higher education, ranking Michigan eighth among the fifty states in total dollar support, twenty-third among the states in appropriations per capita, and thirtieth in state appropriations per $1,000 of personal income (Hines, 1996a).

This support for higher education has been partially offset by the high tuition of Michigan's four-year public universities. Over the past fifteen years, Michigan has consistently ranked among the ten most expensive states in tuition charged by public universities. In FY 1994, Michigan ranked as the ninth most expensive state in the nation in public university tuition charges, with in-state tuition charges at the state's fifteen universities averaging $3,729, as against a national average of $2,689 (U.S. Department of Education, 1984, 1991, 1995).

While the high tuition at the public institutions would seem to offset affordability, Michigan's lower-cost community colleges, a sound state assistance program for students, and each institution's own financial aid packages have continued to ensure a higher level of enrollment. Moreover, Michigan institutions continue to attract as many out-of-state students as are exported to neighboring states. (U.S. Department of Education, 1995).

Finally, the state and its institutions have made considerable attempts to foster ethnic diversity in the student population. Although there is considerable variation among institutions, the percentage of minority undergraduate enrollment in research universities is approximately 30 percent, in public master's and doctoral universities it exceeds 15 percent, and in community colleges it is over 18 percent (U.S. Department of Education, 1993). This compares with a minority population in the state of about 19 percent (U.S. Bureau of the Census, 1995). In addition to institutional programs and initiatives, the state's Chavez Parks King program supports minority initiatives in all public institutions.

State-Level Guidance and Autonomy

State-level coordination or governance of postsecondary education in Michigan is best understood as a loosely structured guidance system rather than a formally coordinated or controlled system. The process of informal state-level guidance is accomplished through the dynamics of constitutional revision, legislation, annual appropriations, litigation, and political influence. To understand this process, it is useful to know the key entities or actors.

Michigan's constitution, the key element in the state-guidance process, recognizes the governing boards of the state's public universities as autonomous, constituting a "fourth estate" free of any direct legislative or state regulatory control. The governing boards of the three research universities are elected directly by the voters in partisan statewide elections. The governing boards of the other ten public universities are appointed by the governor. Each of the twenty-nine community colleges also has its own locally elected governing board. In the absence of a state coordinating or governing body for higher education, each institution can and does address its own concerns about legislation and its appropriation directly to the governor's office and the appropriate legislative committee.

The governor's office, the governor's budget office, and the legislature are also key actors. The governor can initiate legislation and annually initiates the state budget. The governor has one aide devoted explicitly to higher education policy issues and a number of budget analysts whose work focuses on formulating an annual higher education budget. In the legislature, the Senate and House appropriations committees play a preeminent role in state higher education policy formulation. Although the Michigan legislature does have a House Higher Education Committee and a Senate Education Committee, the constitutional status of the public universities drastically limits the policymaking role of these authorizing committees. Rather, the appropriations committees use the power of the purse to influence institutional policy indirectly. Given the power to initiate, modify, approve or defeat, and sign or veto legislative and appropriation bills, these legislative and executive entities are clearly key figures in the state governance and policy process.

Although Michigan lacks a state higher education agency, it does have an elected eight-member State Board of Education to oversee the State Department of Education. However, the board is primarily focused on K–12 education and has only limited responsibilities for higher education, such as collecting information on academic programs and licensing nondegree vocational-technical and proprietary institutions in the state. The board also houses the Michigan Higher Education Assistance Authority, which serves as the state's student assistance agency (McGuinness, 1994). In addition to these quite limited formal powers, the influence of the Department of Education is further reduced since it historically employed few full-time staff devoted to higher education and recently has experienced state budget cuts, which have consolidated and eliminated positions. Consequently the governor's staff and those of the key legislative and fiscal committees are the primary analytic resource for legislative and appropriation hearings.

Three voluntary postsecondary organizations designed to represent the interests of higher education to state government and to mediate potentially divisive differences among the institutions have also emerged. The Presidents' Council of the State Universities of Michigan (originally, the Michigan Council of State College Presidents), founded in 1952, consists of the presidents of the thirteen public universities. The council has a full-time executive director in the state capitol. The presidents meet regularly to discuss varied legislative and appropriation issues. The council also facilitates periodic meetings by the universities' academic and fiscal officers and other senior-level administrative staff for the purpose of reviewing institutional plans to offer new or expanded academic program offerings. In addition, the council conducts peer reviews for new academic programs proposed by the public universities. Programs that are approved by the council are included in the boilerplate language of the legislature's higher education appropriations bill. Institutions that offer nonapproved programs may legally do so, albeit at the risk of legislative reprisal.

Similar associations representing the interests of the community college and the independent college sectors also exist. The Michigan Community College Association, founded in 1970, is a dues-based membership organization that serves as a legislative advocate for community college issues. The Association of Independent Colleges and Universities, founded in 1967, represents over fifty-nine private colleges and universities in the state. Both groups have their own executive director and office in the state capitol.

The Nature of Autonomy

Given Michigan's tradition of deregulation, its constitutional provisions, and its independently elected governing boards for some universities, its institutions have substantial formal autonomy to develop their own missions, govern their own programs and standards, and manage their own admissions and enrollments, revenues and expenditures, and facilities and staffing patterns. They operate in a highly competitive marketplace, competing among themselves for appropriations and with all other postsecondary institutions for other revenues, programs, and enrollments. This competitive marketplace, however, is not without governmental influence and some informal modes of cooperation and coordination.

Institutions are not completely free of state laws, which apply to all public institutions of the state. The state's constitution can be revised either by a state constitutional convention or by legislative amendment. Legislation often applies indirect constraints or introduces conflicts among state constitutional provisions and may engender litigation from the institutions. Appropriations with threats of reductions or promises of increases can be powerful influences.

In sum, Michigan's comprehensive system of postsecondary education, its strong and competitive public sector, its limited state-level coordinating or governing mechanisms, and its autonomous institutions make it an exemplary deregulated state. However, that does not mean the institutions are free of state influence or continuing attempts at coordination and control, or that autonomy is easily maintained.

A Tradition of Constitutional Autonomy and Litigation

Michigan's first state constitution in 1835 established the University of Michigan as the first public university but left the authority for higher education in the hands of the legislature, including the power to control the appointment of regents and professors, establish or abolish academic departments, and manage expenditures (Cudlip, 1969). When early efforts to build the University of Michigan into a strong institution failed, delegates to the state's second constitutional convention, in 1850, met with the intention of changing the constitution to free the university from political interference by the governor and the legislature.

Provisions written into the constitution established the University of Michigan as an independent constitutional corporation under the control of a Board of Regents elected directly by the people, making the university the nation's first constitutionally autonomous public university (Glenny and Dalglish, 1973). The constitution's new language read, "The Board of Regents shall have the general supervision of the University and the direction and control of all expenditures from the University interest fund" (Article XIII, sec. 7). It has been argued that this provision of the 1850 Constitution represents the most important policy decision in the history of Michigan higher education, for the creation of a constitutionally autonomous University of Michigan has remained virtually unchanged, and its model of governance has been extended to other public universities in the state (Laird, 1972).

Shortly after the University of Michigan's constitutional recognition, there began a continuous tradition of litigation brought before the Michigan courts attempting either to constrain the university's autonomy or to defend it from state incursion. Among the numerous cases in the last half of the nineteenth century, two in particular served to define the relative authority of the legislature and the university clearly. In the 1856 case of *Drake* v. *Regents of the University of Michigan* and the 1896 case of *Sterling* v. *University of Michigan Regents*, the court determined that the legislature did not have the authority to dictate academic policies—in these cases, the establishment of professorships—to the University of Michigan through statute. In the landmark *Sterling* decision, which revisited issues addressed in the *Drake* case, the Michigan supreme court wrote that so clear was the 1850 convention's intent regarding the autonomy of public universities that "there was not a single utterance by any member of that convention from which it could be inferred that the members believed or supposed that they were leaving the control of that institution to the legislature." The language in the *Sterling* decision has frequently been used to assert that the Board of Regents, having derived its powers from the same constitution as the legislature, is a fourth coequal branch of government (Cudlip, 1969).

Delegates who convened to draft Michigan's third state constitution in 1908 were so well satisfied with the functioning of the University of Michigan that they decided to confer constitutional status on the recently established Michigan Agricultural College (now Michigan State University) as well (Cudlip, 1969). Despite the new constitution's support for the autonomy of the universities, the next fifty years represented a period of intensive judicial involvement in interpreting the exact nature of this autonomy. With issues relating to the substantive nature of autonomy largely settled by earlier court decisions, the first several decades of the twentieth century witnessed a series of cases in which the courts were asked to decide on procedural issues, revolving essentially around the legality of particular conditions placed on legislative appropriations to the universities. In four key decisions, Michigan courts held that the manner in which institutional funds may be spent was entirely at the universities' discretion and that although the legislature has the authority to attach conditions to funds appropriated for university use, such conditions cannot conflict with the constitutional rights of the universities over their internal academic or fiscal affairs *(Board of Regents of the University of Michigan* v. *Auditor General,* 1911; *Bauer* v. *State Board of Agriculture,* 1911; *State Board of Agriculture* v. *Auditor General,* 1914; *State Board of Agriculture* v. *Auditor General,* 1924).

Momentum for a fourth constitutional convention began to build during the late 1950s in response to the state's worsening economic situation. In 1960, a blue-ribbon commission recommended the establishment of independent institutional governing boards of control for all public colleges and universities and a statewide planning agency to coordinate public higher education. Delegates believed that the governance structure for the state's four regional universities, originally established at the turn of the century as normal schools and still governed by a state board of education, no longer reflected the schools' expanding role as rapidly growing regional universities. Delegates, however, were also concerned about the rapid expansion of the state's higher education system, which they believed was resulting in costly program duplication (Gill, 1987). Thus, two seemingly incongruent issues dominated the discussions on higher education: institutional autonomy and centralized state planning

In a compromise, the Constitution of 1963 extended constitutional status formerly enjoyed only by the University of Michigan, MSU, and Wayne State University to the other four-year public universities. In addition, the new constitution created an eight-member State Board of Education to serve as "the general planning and coordinating body for all public education, including higher education" (Article 8, sec. 3). The ambiguity created by these potentially conflicting provisions of expanded autonomy and a call for increased coordination became the basis for legal action that continued throughout the 1960s, eventually culminating in the state supreme court's 1975 "Salmon decision," which held that the State Board of Education had no substantive authority over the state's constitutionally autonomous public universities.

Issues related to the procedural autonomy of the universities have again been the source of a number of important court cases since the fourth constitutional convention of 1963. These cases reflect the changing nature and increased complexity of the state–higher education relationship in Michigan, and they illustrate the legislature's varied and repeated attempts to regulate the state's "autonomous" universities. In essence, the courts have affirmed the universities' constitutional authority to manage the expenditure of institutional funds, set tuition rates, and determine residency status for the exclusive purpose of deciding tuition rates (*Sprik* v. *Regents of the University of Michigan,* 1972; *Regents of the University of Michigan* v. *State of Michigan,* 1973; *Schmidt* v. *Regents of the University of Michigan,* 1975; *Board of Regents of the University of Michigan* v. *State of Michigan,* 1975).

Thus, the State of Michigan has a long tradition of constitutional autonomy and a history of litigation and court decisions to refine and define it. Since requirements for changing the constitution are matters for a state constitutional convention, which is seldom held, or constitutional amendment, which requires a two-thirds vote of the legislature, issues of conflict over autonomy, coordination, and control have typically been played out in the courts, although largely under the leadership of the University of Michigan and occasionally MSU.

Voluntary Coordination: The Role of the Presidents and the Presidents' Council

As voluntary coordination failed in most states in the 1950s and 1960s, a pattern established in Michigan at that time has played a critical role in limiting conflicts among and between public universities and between the universities and the legislature. The tradition of constitutional autonomy and the balanced development of a comprehensive system of institutions provided a stable base for cooperation, and key leadership within this group has allowed it to remain a viable, if less visible, body.

During the 1950s and 1960s, the university presidents' belief in the need for a voluntary approach to planning and coordination of higher education led to the creation of the Michigan Council of State College Presidents in February 1952. Initially the organization provided a forum for the university presidents to discuss strategies for meeting the state's rapidly increasing enrollment demands and to minimize the impact of negative publicity brought about by previous public debates with one another. Over the years, the Presidents' Council has served three chief functions: (1) collecting and disseminating information, (2) mediating conflict among the universities, and (3) serving as a buffer against creeping state regulation.

The council's early years were marked by disagreement between the two most influential members on its primary policy direction. President John Hannah of Michigan State College campaigned for a legislative agenda that had as its primary goal the acquisition of construction funds for the state's four-year institutions. President Harlan Hatcher of the University of Michigan, fearful that the council would appear merely as a lobbying entity, insisted the council first develop a comprehensive statewide academic plan (Gill, 1987). Unable to reconcile these competing views, the Presidents' Council agreed on an agenda of academic program research aimed at providing needed information regarding Michigan's postsecondary education needs to the institutions and the legislature. During the 1950s, the council sponsored the publication of seven important statewide studies on the condition of higher education in Michigan, focusing on issues of foremost importance to the institution presidents: the state's economic growth, enrollment demands, financial needs, extension services, and graduate and professional education (Chambers, 1961).

The late 1950s and 1960s witnessed intense conflict among the universities as individual institutions undertook aggressive expansion campaigns involving institutional mergers and the development of branch campuses throughout the state. This interinstitutional conflict provoked great irritation among lawmakers, who began demanding new statewide studies of higher education and discussing the need for a state coordinating agency for higher education.

Concern among the presidents regarding state regulation reemerged during the ratification of Michigan's 1963 Constitution. Convention delegates, concerned about unregulated expansion of the state's higher education system, favored the creation of a statewide coordinating board responsible for academic program review. Fearful of the creation of a single governing board with powerful planning and coordinating authority, in December 1961 the Presidents' Council voted to create the Michigan Coordinating Council for Public Higher Education, a new entity whose purpose was to strengthen voluntary coordination through preparation of needs assessment studies, submission of consolidated annual budgets to the legislature, and adoption of a new internal program review process whereby each institution would submit institutional plans to the council when modifying or offering new academic programs (Gill, 1987).

Despite the efforts of the Presidents' Council to forestall the creation of a statewide coordinating board, many lawmakers, convention delegates, and some of the presidents believed that a state board of control located in the Department of Education was preferable to continued legislative interference (Gill, 1987). With the institutional presidents divided on the issue, the proposal to establish a statewide regulatory agency was approved. Michigan's new Constitution of 1963 created an eight-member State Board of Education to serve as "the general planning and coordinating body for all public education, including higher education" (Article 8, sec. 3). Convention delegates, pleased with the excellent academic reputation and governance arrangement enjoyed by the University of Michigan, MSU, and Wayne State University, extended constitutional autonomy to the state's other four-year public universities. Delegates were seemingly blind to the apparent contradiction of extending "autonomy" to other universities while at the same time creating a statewide coordinating board.

Fearful that the new State Board of Education would become involved in institutional budgeting, the Presidents' Council continued to work on the development of a unified budget throughout the 1960s, and for their efforts the universities were rewarded with increases in state appropriations. However, support for an expanded coordinating role for the Department of Education continued to grow among many influential leaders in the state capitol. In 1965, the legislatively created Citizens Committee on Higher Education released its final report, which called for the Department of Education to serve as the central planning and coordinating body for all of higher education in the state (Governor's Commission on the Future of Higher Education, 1984b). The following year, Governor George Romney directed the state budget office to refer all institutional budget requests for new programs to the state board for evaluation and recommendation.

These developments caused great alarm among many of the presidents (Gill, 1987). In 1967, the University of Michigan began legal action intended to clarify the exact nature of the Department of Education's authority and to prevent the state from requiring universities to submit requests for academic programs to the state. This effort was eventually joined by MSU and Wayne State University, and it culminated in the 1975 *Regents of the University of Michigan v. State of Michigan* decision, popularly known as the Salmon decision, after the trial court judge whose opinion was affirmed by the court.

This decision spoke to two important issues: (1) whether the State Board of Education had approval authority for new academic programs at public universities, and (2) whether the legislature had the authority to direct the use of funds appropriated to the three research universities. The state supreme court found in favor of the universities, upholding a broad interpretation of constitutional autonomy and ruling that the board of education was merely an advisory board and had no real authority over the constitutionally autonomous public universities. The court nevertheless aptly observed that the universities needed to realize that the legislature's power of the purse gives the state the ultimate power of persuasion.

In the early 1980s, worsening economic conditions in Michigan indirectly strengthened university autonomy by placing increased emphasis on the market responsiveness of the state's universities. The decline of the automobile industry led to an economic malaise, and in response Governor James Blanchard embarked on a bold program of economic development. The governor and the legislature began to look increasingly to the state's research universities as an engine of economic growth and development and initiated a program of research grants intended to stimulate economic growth through university-based research and development initiatives. Although conflict between the state and the universities continued over a few particularly contentious issues, such as university tuition policy, the governor and leading legislators' belief was that university discretion over matters of internal resource allocation and academic specialization, combined with a state-oriented program of high-technology transfer, would boost institutional market competitiveness and attract new industry to Michigan.

Two challenges currently face the Presidents' Council. First, the decidedly Republican shift in the state capitol has presented new challenges for the council's political strategy. A strong Republican governor, supported by a Republican majority in both House and Senate, has compromised the ability of the universities to exploit political differences among elected officials, especially as some member institutions have used the new political landscape to promote their own legislative agendas. Second, the existence of new instructional technologies presents new problems and challenges to voluntary coordination and threatens to reignite the interinstitutional turf controversies of previous decades.

Recent Legislation and Appropriations Struggles: The Battlefield over Autonomy

Despite the formal grant of university autonomy provided in the constitution, the tradition of voluntary coordination, and the landmark 1975 Salmon decision, which ensured that universities would remain free from regulation by the State Board of Education, the relationship of higher education with state government over the past two decades is replete with efforts by the legislature and governor to influence and control institutional policy. Indeed, in the absence of formal, state-level regulatory structures, the annual legislative session, and especially the appropriations process, have become the vehicles through which the state attempts to exert control over the constitutionally autonomous universities. Five issues—equity in state funding of higher education, university tuition setting, nonresident university enrollments, the open-meetings law and presidential searches, and the regental selection process—portray the continuing controversy between the universities and the state.

Equity in State Funding of Higher Education

State funding for Michigan's public universities is based on a lump-sum, incremental budgeting approach in which the prior year's appropriation for each institution serves as the base to which some percentage increase, with occasional institutional adjustments for special circumstances, is made. Over the years, numerous formulaic approaches to the distribution of state appropriations among the universities have been devised by both the legislature and the governor, including the House Fiscal Agency's 1973 Owen-Huffman Formula Funding Model and the Investment Needs Model, developed in 1984 by the blue-ribbon Governor's Commission on the

Future of Higher Education in Michigan (Governor's Commission on the Future of Higher Education in Michigan, 1984a). Neither model was implemented due to a lack of computer capacity and political will.

During the mid- to late 1980s, Governor James Blanchard called for the adoption of a formula to distribute funds among the universities in response to 8 to 21 percent tuition increases announced by the universities. Campus leaders, and some legislators as well, feared that such a formula would be used to award increased appropriations to universities with low tuition rates and thus serve as a mechanism for the direction of university tuition policy by the legislature (Schwarz, 1994). Ultimately this formula proposal was dropped as the universities voluntarily reined in their own tuition charges and an election brought a new governor into office.

Despite the many formula-based proposals over the years, formula funding does not enjoy unanimous support within the legislature. Some legislators believe that formula approaches to funding Michigan universities are inferior to a fair political process that takes into account the various nuances of individual universities and their conditions.

The use of an incremental, lump-sum appropriation approach makes Michigan universities among the least regulated in the nation with regard to the means of financial control and oversight, but it also means that the universities are particularly vulnerable to political interference during the legislative appropriations process. Until recently, there has been little variation among the universities in the percentage increase in appropriations received annually from the state. Contributing chiefly to this stability is a long tradition of relative cooperation among the universities during the annual legislative appropriations process. The University of Michigan, MSU, and Wayne State University, in particular, have made great efforts to cooperate with one another during the legislative appropriations process, largely out of fear of future reprisal by political allies of the offended institutions. This institutional cooperation was buttressed by a strong system of "patron saintism" in which all three universities enjoyed sponsorship by at least several powerful legislators intent on making sure the universities were treated relatively equally during the legislative appropriations process. This combination of incremental budgeting, cooperation among the universities, and balance in representation of institutional political interests within the legislature, while not always pleasing everyone, treated all relatively the same and therefore left no one completely out.

The 1995 legislative session, however, represented a distinct departure from this tradition and signaled a period of institutional infighting of historic proportions. In December 1994, Governor John Engler proposed a 1995–1996 higher education budget that provided large increases in funding for MSU (7.5 percent), Grand Valley State University (6 percent), and Western Michigan University (7.8 percent), while the other ten public universities, including the University of Michigan, were allotted only small 3 percent rate-of-inflation adjustments. The governor's rationale for the differential funding proposal was that the three universities had been historically underfunded. Three other interrelated factors, however, were also largely responsible for the governor's budget recommendations.

The proposed funding differential most likely reflects recent dramatic shifts in the Michigan political landscape. In recent years, Republicans have risen to ascendancy in both House and Senate, shifting power away from the previously dominant and more Democratic Detroit and southeast Michigan area and toward the more conservative western and northern portions of the state. A second, closely related change is the increasing political strength of MSU in the state legislature. With but a few exceptions, the leadership in both the Michigan House and Senate are MSU graduates, prompting one prominent Republican senator to observe that the "brightest, smartest, and politically strongest" members of the Republican caucus are almost all Michigan State alumni.

Finally, Governor Engler's historic 1995–1996 higher education budget can also be partially explained by the aggressive legislative lobbying efforts of MSU's new president, M. Peter McPherson. McPherson, a former banking executive and Reagan administration official with no former experience in higher education, was selected for the MSU presidency in August 1993 after a highly publicized and controversial search process in which Governor Engler, an MSU graduate, was reported to have influenced the board's decision. McPherson quickly unveiled a mandate concentrating more on undergraduate students, reducing university spending growth, and keeping higher education accessible and affordable—messages warmly received in the legislature and in the press. McPherson also began to lobby the legislature vigorously for increased funding. MSU's position was greatly strengthened when just weeks before the start of the legislative session, McPherson announced that for the next three years, MSU would limit tuition hikes to no more than the rise in the consumer price index. While publicly claiming that the move was not intended as a "negotiating" stance with the legislature, MSU clearly hoped that the state would respond with appropriations sufficient to cover any lost revenue. Two weeks later, in what has been described by a number of both Democratic and Republican leading legislators as a political deal, Governor Engler reaffirmed his support for the differential appropriations increase for the three universities.

The appropriations issue made the 1995 legislative session one of the most intensive institutional lobbying campaigns in the history of Michigan higher education. Despite grave warnings from University of Michigan and Wayne State University presidents that MSU's aggressive lobbying would harm the relations among the universities, McPherson refused to defer Michigan State's short-term interests to a presumed greater good. Only in the final days of the legislative session, and due to the almost single-handed efforts of the Senate higher education appropriations subcommittee chairman, a prominent University of Michigan backer, did the legislature concede to enacting a supplemental appropriation for the University of Michigan–led coalition of institutions—one, however, that would not take effect until the following year—while at the same time leaving intact the 7 percent range increases for MSU, Grand Valley State, and Western Michigan University.

Tuition Setting

Although the Michigan courts ruled two decades ago that the universities have the exclusive power to establish tuition rates, the legislature and the governor have continued to attempt to influence public university tuition policy. Today this issue remains one of the more contentious in the state-university relationship. Throughout the 1980s, the public universities' double-digit-percentage annual tuition increases and the state's severe economic downturn made issues of college affordability and accessibility a central component of Governor James Blanchard's higher education agenda, and he mounted a vigorous campaign to bring public pressure to bear against the universities. In 1983 and 1984, for example, his blue-ribbon Commission on the Future of Higher Education released a series of reports that called attention to the high tuition charges of Michigan universities. The governor also repeatedly threatened to withhold funding from institutions that refused to suppress tuition increases.

In 1986, with support from the legislature, Governor Blanchard created the Michigan Educational Trust (MET). MET, the nation's first "prepaid" college tuition program, provided investors with the opportunity to pay college tuition in advance at any one of the state's four-year public institutions. Conflict arose between the universities and the governor when it was learned that the actuarial projections MET's financial advisers used in calculating the price for future prepayment contracts assumed annual tuition increases far below actual increases of recent years. University leaders claimed that by tying the financial integrity of the MET program to artificially low and "unrealistic" tuition projections, the governor and legislature were attempting to dictate university tuition policy indirectly.

In the first year of MET's existence, FY 1989, officials projected a 9 percent increase in tuition at Michigan's public universities several weeks before the universities themselves announced tuition increases of between 8 percent and 21 percent, with a system average of 13.5 percent. When the universities announced their own planned tuition increases, the governor accused them of breaking the MET and threatened to veto the appropriation of any university that did not lower its tuition increase to under 10 percent (Schwarz, 1994).

The tuition issue reemerged during the 1995 legislative session when a bill was introduced into the House of Representatives aimed at rewarding colleges and universities that held tuition increases to a minimum. The legislation, entitled the Higher Education and Job Skills Tax Bill, offered a tax deduction for families who paid college tuition at any public two- or four-year college or university in Michigan, but after the first year, the deduction was valid only for those who attended an institution that held tuition at or below the rate of inflation. The bill, developed by the Senate

Republican Caucus, was sponsored by the Senate majority leader, who stated that the intent of the bill was to "send a message to state colleges and universities that unbridled tuition increases must come to an end" (Posthumus, 1995). Some legislators viewed the tax deduction proposal as a stroke of genius. One Senate leader reported that his colleagues believed they had "finally found the hammer" that would allow the legislature to dictate institutional tuition policy.

University leaders recognized they were in a politically tenuous position: passage of the bill could mean significant financial losses and a usurpation of the universities' tuition-setting prerogative, but opposition to it could make the universities look as if they supported the idea of high tuition. The universities, through the Michigan Council of State College Presidents, campaigned against the tax deduction proposal, eventually whittling it down to a deduction of 4 percent of college tuition, up to $250.

Enrollments

Another recurring issue related to the battle for autonomy is control over institutional enrollments, particularly the resident-nonresident enrollment ratio of the University of Michigan's undergraduate and professional schools, which enroll far greater percentages of nonresident students than do the state's other public universities. Nonresident undergraduate enrollment at the University of Michigan has crept as high as 35 percent, and nonresident enrollment at some of the professional schools is in the 50 to 60 percent range. This has long been a source of conflict between the university and the legislature, many of whose members resent the state's subsidization of large numbers of nonresident students in Michigan universities. In response, the legislature has occasionally threatened punitive appropriations action. Such action was threatened during the 1987 legislative session, when it was alleged that the University of Michigan was admitting high numbers of out-of-state students in an attempt to compensate for lost tuition revenues resulting from the tuition control measures imposed by Governor Blanchard. A negotiated compromise restored the threatened appropriations when the university agreed to report the mix of resident and nonresident students periodically to a legislative committee (Schwarz, 1994). As part of this informal understanding with the legislature, the University of Michigan agreed to hold the nonresident undergraduate enrollment at or below the 30 percent level.

The enrollment issue reemerged during the 1995 legislative session when, at the height of the appropriations conflict between MSU and the University of Michigan–led coalition of institutions, one legislator revealed that the University of Michigan's nonresident undergraduate enrollment had climbed to 34 percent, in violation of the earlier agreement between the university and the legislature. The higher education budget bill was quickly amended, making the University of Michigan's proposed 3 percent appropriations increase for 1995–1996 (approximately $8.3 million) conditional on the university's promise to keep its nonresident student population at no more than 30 percent. Campus officials responded that they believed the 1987 agreement had been only temporary in nature and that the punitive appropriations action was an orchestrated attempt to embarrass the university before the legislature and to divert its attention from pressuring the governor and legislators to increase its appropriations. They noted that the legislature had known for several years that the number of nonresident students had moved above the 30 percent mark but had not lodged a complaint until this time.

The University of Michigan's public handling of the issue was widely reported as damaging to the institution's political standing in the legislature. Ultimately the appropriation was restored in the closing weeks of the legislative session, and the university accepted several hundred additional first-year resident undergraduate students, thereby reducing the nonresident student proportion of its undergraduate student enrollment to approximately 30 percent.

Open Meetings and Presidential Searches

The applicability of the state of Michigan's open-meetings law to college and university presidential searches has served as a recent source of strain between the universities and the state's print media. This issue has centered on striking an appropriate balance between the public's right to information and the universities' responsibility to govern themselves under the state constitution.

In September 1993, the Michigan Supreme Court sided with the *Ann Arbor News* and the *Detroit Free Press*, ruling that the University of Michigan had broken the state's open-meetings law during its 1988 search for a new president (Cole, 1993). Soon after, a state appellate court ruled that MSU had also violated state law when it conducted elements of its presidential search behind closed doors.

This controversy has beset numerous other universities and community colleges over the openness of their searches. Wayne County Community College, for example, reopened its presidential search in January 1995 after the *Detroit News* and *Free Press* sued the school for conducting secret meetings to talk about candidates. Following the fall 1995 announcement of the resignation of James Duderstadt as president of the University of Michigan, effective July 1, 1996, the University of Michigan Board of Regents was urged by various groups to establish a complex search process using consultants and an advisory committee to screen candidates. In November 1996, following a rigorous search process, Dartmouth College provost Lee C. Bollinger, a former dean of the University of Michigan Law School, was selected as the university's twelfth president. As in previous searches, however, several of the state's newspapers sued the university under the state's Open Meetings Act, challenging the university's process. In fact, the University of Michigan paid nearly $225,000 to outside attorneys to help the school comply with the act and to defend it against the newspapers' suits (Hoover, 1997).

Future presidential searches in Michigan may not incur such a hefty financial and political burden. In response to growing bipartisan consensus that some modification of the state law as it pertains to universities was both appropriate and necessary to ensure a supply of quality presidential candidates for Michigan institutions, in 1997 the state legislature passed an amendment to the Open Meetings Act, allowing universities to meet privately and keep confidential the names of candidates until the list is narrowed to five finalists.

Trustee and Regent Selection

Following the surprise resignation of University of Michigan president James Duderstadt in September 1995, the regental selection process of the University of Michigan, MSU, and Wayne State University came under public fire by Governor John Engler. Under the Michigan Constitution, board members at these three universities are popularly elected through partisan statewide elections. Governor

Engler, despite Duderstadt's own claims to the contrary, asserted the president had been pushed out of office by "petty" board members who failed to receive the kind of "care and feeding" they thought they should receive. Other observers viewed the governor's public outrage as contrived for the purpose of raising an old debate over the regental selection process of the three universities to gain greater state control over regental appointment to the autonomous universities or to boost his own national political stature in a presidential election year.

Although there is some support for changing the regental selection process from elective to gubernatorial appointment at the three research universities, such a change would require an amendment to the state constitution, and, according to numerous leading politicians and university trustees, it would engender concerted opposition and is considered extremely unlikely. Moreover, support for the idea even among the governor's allies is tentative at best.

As these issues suggest, in a state with limited state-level regulation, the legislative and appropriations processes reflect continued attempts to influence institutions and are a source of continuing conflict between state government and its higher educational institutions. Sometimes there are winners and losers, often coalitions and compromises, and occasionally new court cases on constitutional issues. The Presidents' Council, the key legislative and executive committees, varying coalitions, and key individuals (presidents, governors, and former legislators) all have influence. But the processes are open, fluid, and occasionally turbulent.

Lessons from an Unregulated State

Clearly Michigan, like many other states, has its own unique history in the emergence and development of its system of higher educational institutions. An early and continuous tradition of institutional autonomy, a high degree of public support for higher education, and expansion during periods of population growth and prosperity were important factors in developing a comprehensive, high-quality system with little state regulation. The state's mix of political and institutional leadership over the past four decades has tolerated the diverse tensions and made voluntary coordination survive while it has withered in other states. The ongoing struggles that are played out in legislation, appropriations, and judicial conflicts are a critical and continuing part of the story. It is difficult as well as dangerous to draw lessons from a single state; however, in a context of comparison with other more regulated states and as useful advice to those contemplating deregulation, the following insights from the Michigan case are useful hypotheses, if not clear guidelines:

- It is possible to build a strong, comprehensive system of public higher education in an unregulated state. Michigan's experience with autonomy, however, is characterized by a long history of legal, political, and popular support in a state whose higher education system matured during periods of state growth and economic prosperity; the consequences of moving from a highly regulated to a less-regulated environment are less clear.

- Institutions in a deregulated system need to be competitively oriented regarding the acquisition of programs, students, and resources, and they need to build the administrative structures required to accomplish that.

- The absence of a state-level governing or coordinating body responsible for mediating conflict between state and institution officials engaged in an often turbulent political environment can result in a tight coupling, whereby the vicissitudes of the larger state political environment can quickly affect the fortunes of individual institutions. A well-developed state and legislative relations staff at the institutional level is indispensable.

- Constitutional autonomy may or may not guarantee more stability than statutory autonomy, but it probably has more symbolic value. The constitutional basis for autonomy can promote a political culture that institutionalizes respect for autonomy and provides some measure of insulation from political interference. A tradition of constitutional autonomy, reinforced by litigation and judicial interpretation, provides a strong framework for state-institution relations but does not eliminate conflict.

- The tension that exists between autonomy and accountability requires a significant investment of energy in dealing with continuous crises and conflicts between higher education's interests and state-level concerns. Litigation to defend autonomy is costly and time-consuming and can bring other political or financial retribution.

Moreover, in an era of sagging public confidence in higher education, litigation intended to protect institutional autonomy can appear arrogant in the face of the state's seemingly well-intentioned desire to improve accountability.

• Between infrequent constitutional revisions and major court cases, the legislative and appropriations processes become primary arenas in which state policymakers seek to achieve some modicum of state coordination and control.

• Voluntary coordination among institutions is critical in an unregulated setting and can serve to advance a common, unified message on behalf of higher education, mediate conflict among the institutions, and buffer institutions from political intrusion by the state. Voluntary coordination, however, requires institutional leadership that values autonomy more than state control, is committed to making it work, and has a statewide perspective rather than a narrow focus on institutional interests. One potential disadvantage of the voluntarily coordinated system is the unequal benefits accruing to, and demands placed on, the institutions. Although the larger and more politically powerful institutions may derive the greatest benefits from the system, these institutions also incur the greatest legal, financial, and political burdens associated with defending it.

• Major studies and commissions that address important statewide issues—whether initiated by the governor, the legislature, or a voluntary board—are helpful in focusing all parties on that issue as a priority. These studies and commissions may serve a more important policy formulation role than in states where formal, state-level authority to regulate higher education exists.

The primary lesson from the Michigan example is that in a deregulated environment, the struggles between state demand for accountability and institutional claims for autonomy do not dissipate. They merely take a different pattern and are subject to their own set of dynamics: a fluid interplay among competition, cooperation, conflict, and coordination. There is a need for institutions in a deregulated state to value competition yet find means to cooperate on statewide issues. There is a continuous conflict between institutional concern for maintaining autonomy and the state's press for accountability and control. State coordination is expressed in constant struggles over legislation and appropriations issues and the ongoing legal battles between the state and its institutions to clarify their constitutional autonomy. Maintaining an appropriate level of institutional cooperation and statewide coordination in the midst of a competitive and occasionally conflictual environment is a dynamic system requiring continuous attention by institutions and state leaders.

Chapter Nine

Implementing Independence: Benefits and Obligations

Terrence J. MacTaggart

When asked his opinion on the value of Western civilization, Mahatma Gandhi is said to have replied, "I think it is a good idea. We should try it." This chapter argues that deregulating public higher education is proving to be a good idea, and states ought to try it much more than they do. A review of the chapters on Maryland, New Jersey, and Michigan, as well as the ideas presented elsewhere in this book, suggests that deregulation works in preserving and sometimes increasing quality and in maintaining access and diversity, although it does not automatically reduce cost. Following a discussion of the conditions that must precede liberalization, the chapter recommends several concrete actions that states might take to capture the advantages of deregulation.

Autonomy Works

If success in deregulation means maintaining or improving academic quality while continuing a progressive agenda of access and diversity, then these experiments in autonomy are successful. The over one hundred years' worth of experience in Michigan, five years of St. Mary's College's experiment, and even the very new experience in New Jersey suggest that greater independence from excessive regulation encourages substantial quality as well as a progressive social agenda. One could argue that institutions in these states would enjoy higher quality and greater minority enrollment if they were more highly regulated to do so, but there is little compelling evidence to support that view. Conversely, it is difficult to assert that autonomy alone caused these benefits. Rather, a combination of able leadership, social and political pressure, and the absence of a stultifying bureaucracy led to positive societal and academic accomplishments. Freedom from excessive control probably offered the opportunity for visionary and competent leaders with adequate resources to achieve better results than they could have in a more constrained world.

By most conventional measures, academic quality at Michigan's institutions runs high, St. Mary's appears to be one of the best of its kind, and in the short time New Jersey has enjoyed independence, there is no sign of reduced standards. Reputational studies consistently rank programs at the University of Michigan and Michigan State University very high; across the state, universities hold regional accreditation and appropriate specialized accreditation; and it is safe to say that most knowledgeable professionals within higher education would give the state high marks for overall quality.

As indicated by entering student test scores and faculty qualifications, the substantial levels of quality at St. Mary's before autonomy have continued to grow. Berdahl points out in Chapter Four that the quality of incoming students continued to improve following St. Mary's charter status. Further, the Middle States accreditation team that visited in 1995 confirmed the quality of the faculty and otherwise attested to St. Mary's academic virtues.

Ardent free marketers would argue that the unconstrained environment in which these institutions operate virtually demands that they exhibit high quality in order to succeed. The reputation for quality certainly bestows market advantages on colleges and universities just as it does in the case of the market for automobiles and candy bars. As we have seen, economists define the market for higher education as monopolistically competitive in that numerous small firms—colleges and universities—compete with one another to a large extent based on the distinct qualities that consumers believe to inhere in the product or service. The more attractive and unique the image, the greater the market power and ability to garner more customers and charge them a higher price. This theory largely explains why Ivy League colleges can charge the highest tuitions and community colleges the lowest. The argument continues that all institutions, whatever their status, would be motivated in a free-market world to become and be perceived as qualitatively distinct as possible in order to receive the rewards the monopolistic competition offers.

But before we attribute too much goodwill or good sense to the invisible hand of the market, recall that the institutions studied here, and most others, are far from free of external oversight on the quality front. St. Mary's must still report assessments of student learning to the state coordinating board, and all the institutions are subject to accreditation review. Substantial reductions in perceived quality would jeopardize the college's coveted freedom from state control. Presumably this serves as a powerful if latent motivator. In addition to the incentives provided by academic culture and public expectations, the market clearly rewards quality as well. Yet one only need look at the range of value offered by the relatively free market in proprietary education, which moves from the exemplary to the scandalous, to recognize that the market in the United States permits and even encourages quality, but alone does not ensure it.

The fear that independence would bring with it a focus on wealthy, white students has proved unfounded. While about one of five Michigan residents comes from a minority group, nearly a third of the enrollments at the research universities are minority and about 15 percent at the other public universities and community colleges (see Chapter Eight). In keeping with its compact with the State of Maryland, St. Mary's sustains a modestly increasing minority population, which reached 16 percent of enrollment in 1994 (Berdahl, 1998). The history of minority enrollment in New Jersey reveals that consistent growth in minority enrollment that preceded deregulation has continued with the change (see Chapter Five).

Would this same commitment exist absent the enforcement of state affirmative action policies and strong forces in the legislature representing minority interests? Greer points out in Chapter Five that the National Association for the Advancement of Colored People (NAACP) in New Jersey opposed deregulation, fearing that the commitment to diversity would erode without state intervention. The real threat to diversity is not deregulation, but court judgments striking down race-based admissions policies. Ironically, in the current environment, minority admissions fall when the courts decide not to allow universities the freedom to set admissions criteria.

Freedom Has Its Price

Independence and the benefits it brings come at a price in these wealthy and generous states. In 1996, for example, Michigan ranked in the top ten among the states in total dollar support for higher education: $1.6 billion. A comparison of Michigan's free-market approach with the more restricted governance systems of some other states confirms that costs to Michigan's students and taxpayers run higher (California Higher Education Policy Center, 1997). Yet as a relatively wealthy state, Michigan citizens can afford this largesse. Nevertheless, in spite of this massive total investment in higher education, Michigan falls behind twenty-nine other states in appropriations per $1,000 of personal income (Hines, 1996). New Jersey, the second wealthiest state in the nation when wealth is measured by income per person, ranks in the top ten states by appropriating about $1.2 billion annually to higher education (Greer, Chapter Five). Of course, New Jersey had high costs before the latest deregulation, but there is no sign that the new autonomy will itself lower cost.

St. Mary's College of Maryland has been doing better at garnering state support than the average of its sister institutions within the University of Maryland system. By one calculation, St. Mary's College received nearly 30 percent greater state support in the five years following 1993 than did the Maryland system (Berdahl, Chapter Four). Even after "backing out" funds provided to make up for an earlier shortfall, the college still did better than the system as a whole (Berdahl, Chapter Four). Coupling this relatively generous level of state support with the college's hefty tuition—about $5,500 per student, as opposed to the average for Maryland's comprehensive institutions of $3,000—results in a very well funded public institution. The college's success at raising private dollars further contributes to its very healthy microeconomy.

In economic theory, greater competition reduces cost. Why is this not the case in public higher education? As we have suggested, in the monopolistically competitive arena, higher perceived quality allows the firm (read the university) to charge a higher price. Lost scale economies enjoyed by some efficiently run large systems are a likely additional cause of some of the higher costs. If Michigan chooses to concentrate service functions such as legal counsel, internal audit, payroll, and legislative relations, for example, in one or a few central units, the likely result would be less duplication of these same services at each of the institutions. Zemsky and Massy's well-known "administrative lattice" and "academic ratchet," in which an institution's costs increase because of greater numbers of administrative staff and a leaning toward academic specialization (Pew Higher Education Research Program, 1990), also contribute to the duplication in this state that lacks an authoritative statewide coordinating or governing body that could constrain these impulses. Set against whatever savings tighter coordination and control might bring are the additional transaction costs (Wilson, 1989) of having to respond to a supervising bureaucracy. Finally, and probably most significant, are the costs of fairly large-scale duplication of programs at campuses and in outreach locations across the state.

There is potential for program sprawl in New Jersey as well. It appears that the restraint imposed by the old coordinating board has yielded to log-rolling among members of the new Presidents' Council. Under the new rules, institutional boards can approve new programs that fall within their mission; the Commission on Higher Education and the Presidents' Council become engaged only when the programs are thought to exceed the mission, be too costly, or be unnecessarily duplicative (Greer, Chapter Five). Thus, seventy-three new degree programs have moved forward without, as Greer points out, much controversy—but one might suspect without much scrutiny as well.

If this unconstrained spread of programs creates cost pressures, it also creates more opportunities for consumers. Proponents of the Michigan and New Jersey models prefer to let the market (in this case, the political market, which generates state funding, and the student market, producing tuition revenue) decide which programs will succeed rather than the judgments of a central bureaucracy. The charge to St. Mary's was not to be cheap, but to be good, and it seems to be fulfilling that mandate.

A Changing Context

The original conditions that fostered centralized patterns of managing public higher education, notably rapid growth in enrollment, programs, physical plant, and public investment, have changed. At the same time, new ideas have emerged for addressing the endemic challenges, such as the need to manage, if not resolve, conflicts among growing and declining parts of a state and rivalries among institutions (McGuinness, 1996), which also pushed states toward centralized control systems.

Callan, Bracco, and Richardson in Chapter Six identify five environmental factors that call for different governance schemes from those of the past. They observe these salient challenges: increasing demand in many western and southern states coupled with growing public resistance to paying higher tax bills for more access, rising public concern with the quality and relevance of educational programs along with anxiety over affordability, and the enigmatic but embracive presence of rapidly changing communications technology. These factors are not new on the face of the earth, but never before have they been combined together at one time. Callan and his associates contend that more or less centralized structures (or highly decentralized models for that matter) will not work to manage the current complexity as well as the more flexible federal system that they endorse.

At the same time, while the seemingly "intractable" (McGuinness, 1996, p. 207) pressures toward centralized decision making continue, new ideas have emerged for responding to such perennial concerns as the need to resolve conflicts among institutions and regions of the state, to ensure that student-consumers are protected, and to achieve efficiencies. The history of self-regulation in Michigan illustrates the point that colleges and universities can work reasonably well together to resolve disputes among themselves and to address conflicts between urban and rural parts of the state. New Jersey may develop similar voluntary ways of managing conflicts, although the jury is still out on this question.

When national news magazines regularly feature reports ranking institutions and programs, it is difficult to say that consumers lack access to information to guide their choices. Although there is plenty of dispute over the criteria used in these nationally publicized rankings, there is no doubt that this publicity contributes to consumer awareness of the differences among competing educational options. Steps to inform consumers better and involve them in decisions affecting tuition charges and programs, required as part of the liberalization in New Jersey, are becoming increasingly popular elsewhere. Empowering consumers with better information seems to be a less costly and more effective way of ensuring their interests are met than asking a bureaucracy to look out for them.

Finally, many central administrative functions can be rendered more responsive and efficient if they are demonopolized. As I suggest later in this chapter, allowing campuses to bid on or seek private sources for such common services as building design, computer networking, and legal services reduces the costs of central administrative units.

Although the need for central authority to plan for and regulate expansion, referee disputes among institutions and regions, protect consumers from substandard academic offerings, and provide common administrative services has diminished, it has not disappeared, nor is it likely to. The task ahead is to decide what its central role ought to be in relation to the academy and the larger public and then to reengineer governing structures and relationships to take advantage of the vitality that a freer market promises.

Conditions Favoring Deregulation

Some states favor a more laissez-faire approach to managing public higher education, while others prefer explicit control. The reasons for these preferences lie within the unique political history of each state, and they vary with the ambitions and competence of its political leaders. Yet based on the evidence presented in this book and elsewhere, it is possible to identify some common conditions that need to be in place before a state will shift from a more to a less regulated environment.

Substantial Precedents Favoring Autonomy Help

It is one thing to defend constitutional autonomy successfully, as the universities in Michigan have done so often and so vigorously; it is quite another to gain that independence when so many interest groups find comfort in the status quo. New Jersey's state colleges escaped the control of the coordinating board in part because the relative independence enjoyed by Rutgers and the state's two-year community colleges helped make the case for the state colleges. St. Mary's enjoyed a unique status as the state's public honors college before the restructuring that led to its relative independence.

Independence and Qualitative Distinction

Institutions with truly distinctive missions, reputations, or niches in the marketplace are better positioned to make claims for greater independence. The public Ivys sprinkled across the country are well positioned to capture additional freedom where they do not already possess it, as are those public research and land-grant universities that hold a powerful position in the marketplace.

Extreme Frustration with Existing Oversight Policies and Agencies

It is not hard to find critics of coordinating and governing boards, as well as regulatory agencies, but opposition to what many regard as necessary evils must approach incandescence to support their dissolution. The New Jersey Department of Higher Education had acquired a reputation for authoritarian and arbitrary decision making. So friendless were they, the story goes, that the governor's plans to dissolve the agency were an open secret to everyone but the agency's director.

But even highly intense frustration with regulators presents no guarantee that eliminating them will lead to greater independence for colleges and universities. Illinois, which in 1994 eliminated two of its system boards and offices in favor of institutional boards, nevertheless maintained a strong coordinating board. Minnesota eliminated its coordinating board as part of a larger restructuring but transferred much of its authority to a new governing board, which appears to be exercising closer control of public institutions.

A Political Environment Favoring Autonomy

Politicians have historically preferred to control the academy through the power of the purse or direct legislation rather than rely on the marketplace. As Peterson and McLendon make clear in Chapter Eight, the story of Michigan independence is one of chronic legal warfare between the universities and political forces seeking to restrict their independence. Change came to Maryland not because Governor William Donald Schaefer wanted to set St. Mary's or any other institution free, but because he wanted "someone he could call to get things done" in higher education (Berdahl and Schmidtlein, 1996, p. 165). St. Mary's won its freedom during the long and complicated political process that resulted, ironically, in a system quite different from the one the governor had originally intended (Berdahl and Schmidtlein, 1996). In fact, as studies of restructuring in Minnesota, Alaska, Massachusetts, Maryland, and North Dakota show, when political leaders decide to restructure, it almost always moves in the direction of greater, not less, oversight and regulation (MacTaggart and Associates, 1996). Armed with a strong free-market philosophy and national political ambitions, Governor Whitman's decision to deregulate New Jersey higher education partially remains an exception to national trends.

Wealth

Thus far only relatively wealthy states have endorsed substantial deregulation. New Jersey boasts the second highest per capita income in the country, and Michigan ranks in the top third among states. With few exceptions, poorer states appreciate the economies that regulation and coordination appear to bring over the greater degrees of duplication and choice that are gifts of a free market.

How to Balance Autonomy and the Public Interest

There is much to be learned from the experience with deregulation described in this book and from thinking about the advantages held by leaders in private institutions. What policies would a state choose if it wanted to reap the benefits of deregulation while preserving politically acceptable levels of public control and the advantages of some levels of coordination in reducing costs?

At the outset, policymakers need to understand and accept two seemingly contradictory realities. First, deregulation means just that: transferring meaningful authority from boards or bureaucracies and their staffs to university executives. Second, if deregulation is to be effective, the residual authority of boards and agencies, as well as their expectations for performance, must be clearly and unequivocally established. License without accountability is a recipe for disaster, as a range of examples from the U.S. savings and loan industry to the introduction of a market economy in Russia illustrates.

Without a thorough appreciation of the political costs of transferring authority, well-intentioned deregulators may be in for rude surprises. System trustees, for example, may readily sign up under the banner of granting their university presidents greater management authority in the abstract, but quickly retreat if the exercise of that power includes the discretion to set higher tuition, pay some employees more than system norms, or drastically alter admissions policies. Some policymakers are unwilling to endure the public criticism that comes from letting the market, or an executive's reading of the market potential, dictate bold departures from current, safe practice. Others may believe that in carrying out their responsibility to keep cost down and access up, they must review every new program proposal and tightly control tuition changes. In these instances, prospects for substantial deregulation are slim.

Once policymakers accept a working balance between independence and control, they must identify what they want to achieve by changing the power equation. Encouraging greater competition, creating more responsiveness to markets, decentralizing authority, and so on serve not as ends in themselves, but ought to represent a better way of providing public services than management by rule. As a preface to suggestions on using reduced regulation to achieve better public service, let us suppose a state identifies the following goals for public higher education:

- *Fiscal goals:* Become less reliant on state appropriations through more efficient management, flexibility in setting tuition, and developing alternative sources of revenue
- *Access goals:* Improve access by emphasizing participation of minority and low-income students in proportion to their numbers in the state and by distributing services across the state
- *Distinctive choice goals:* Increase the public's ability to choose from distinct options among public institutions by emphasizing the differing missions of the research campus, the liberal arts college, urban institutions, and a polytechnic university

- *Economic development goals:* Focus the attention and resources of the universities on creating economic opportunity and jobs for the state's citizens

These goals reflect the ambiguities and contradictions inherent in providing services to a public with diverse opinions and preferences. Achieving these goals requires trade-offs. For example, granting tuition flexibility while maintaining high levels of access, even with ingenious financial aid policies, will be controversial. The desire to increase nonstate revenues probably lends itself to a more laissez-faire environment; the charge to unite the universities in the interests of expanding the state's economy seems to call for a fairly high level of central leadership.

The hypothetical board might consider the following ideas to increase campus autonomy and maintain a focus on the public interest.

Give Universities the Freedom to Raise, Reserve, and Spend Money

University systems should change their financing policies to allow each constituent campus to propose its own tuition charges based on mission, program costs, and what the market would bear. Universities would keep all the tuition they generate. To link the authority for financial management with its responsibility, universities would be permitted to carry funds forward from one fiscal year to the next and would receive their board-approved state allocation in a lump sum rather than with line-item restrictions. The institutions might be challenged to increase private fundraising by making such increases part of the performance expectations for presidents and matching private contributions with public monies when, say, the private contributions exceed the prior year's by 10 percent. Presidential compensation could be linked to success in increasing private support.

Link Tuition Hikes to Increased Financial Aid

One of the hallmarks of public higher education is its responsibility to find a place for qualified students whatever their economic resources. Thus, a nonnegotiable requirement for greater tuition flexibility is the demand that a substantial portion of the increase be recycled into financial aid for low-income students.

Exploit Technology to Serve Students and Reduce Costs

As Mingle and Epper point out in Chapter Two, communications technology requires substantial coordinated investment but also creates the opportunity for more flexible educational service to students as well as administrative efficiencies. Too often technology is added on, but processes and the personnel complement do not change. To achieve greater access, courses delivered using technology are available from a variety of sources. The key is that they be integrated into the educational program. On the administrative side, the financial and airline industries offer examples of using technology to deliver widely disbursed services efficiently.

Demonopolize Central Administrative Services

Most public institutions are required to accept certain administrative services from a central agency. This might be a system office or the state's attorney general's office, the department of employee relations for collective bargaining, the department of administration for purchasing, and various facilities bureaus for capital expansion and repair. Although these services often contribute to the scale economies of systems, because of their monopoly status, they can also be unresponsive and costly. To control or reduce both university and system administrative costs, the board might require that all central services currently provided by the system office—computing, facilities management, and so on—be opened to competitive bids from private providers or let on a contract basis to a lead campus. In each instance a "customer council" made up of representatives of the universities using the service would be empowered to set standards for performance and indicate the prices they are willing to pay before going to another vendor. Given the choice, central services provided by a system to its constituent institutions are likely to be more responsive than the same services provided by a state secretariat to every state agency. But even in this case, requiring services that are on a par with those available from the private sector will improve performance and possibly reduce cost.

Create Charter Universities

By virtue of historic strengths and remarkable leadership, some institutions in each state lend themselves to the extra level of independence achieved by St. Mary's of Maryland. This status might accrue to highly specialized universities such as a public Ivy, a polytechnic, or a distinctive nontraditional university. Where such potential exists, the state can grant special freedom from normal oversight in return for a charter that requires that standards of quality, access, and private fundraising be met. The charter might include a separate board or special dispensations under the existing governing board.

Substitute Agreements, Contracts, and Charters for "One Size Fits All" Rules

To support distinctiveness among public institutions, even when full charter status is not practical, leaders must remain vigilant against that oligarchic tendency to apply the same rules to everyone. This is especially critical in collective bargaining, where unions, in the interests of equity, try to bargain up to the institution with the highest compensation and most flexible workload. Whenever possible, the contract must make provision for differing personal practices and performance expectations depending on differing missions. System personnel policies on compensation, promotion, and tenure should also be fluid enough to accommodate and encourage differences among campuses.

Grant More Formal Authority to Consumers and Stakeholders

The struggle facing higher education is the shift from a producer-controlled enterprise to one in which the consumer enjoys greater power. Put another way, deregulation succeeds best when it links the actions of providers directly to the needs of consumers. Ways of engaging students, their parents, and community members include requiring, as New Jersey does, public hearings on proposed tuition hikes and major policy changes, and the active use of strong and influential advisory groups. This democratization of higher education contains some pleasant surprises. For example, when asked to support a tuition hike in return for specific qualitative benefits such as greater access to computers or smaller class size, students often become solid supporters of the investment.

Seek Voluntary and Self-Regulatory Mechanisms of Control over Rules and Mandates

If empowering external stakeholders makes sense, so internal groups such as councils of presidents and alliances among boards deserve the recognition and authority to respond to local concerns. The long-standing Presidents' Council in Michigan and a similar group in New Jersey, along with that state's association of governing boards, show the potential of this brand of voluntary governance.

Reconceive, Then Reengineer System-Campus Relationships

Coordinating and governing boards need to work with campus and state leaders in reimagining their roles in a world that demands greater autonomy at the local level while simultaneously expecting more focused and efficient service from higher education collectively. The "entrepreneurial university-efficient system" model being implemented in Maine illustrates one attempt to reconfigure the partnership among the campus, board, and the state. Maine's public university trustees recognized that state support would continue to be low for the foreseeable future, that the state suffers a dearth of baccalaureate degree holders compared to other New England states, and that it possesses a diverse system. Components include a land-grant university, a growing urban institution, a public liberal arts college, regional campuses in rural areas, and a nontraditional institution with substantial distance-education programs. With all this in mind, the trustees embarked on a consistent effort to reengineer its management and governance practices.

The result has been a devolution of some authority to campus presidents for decisions over tuition rates, faculty salaries, and admissions policies, along with higher expectations for private fundraising. The system office now plays a stronger role in public and legislative advocacy, managing technology, and setting priorities for funding. Telecommunications for distance education and administration are managed as systemwide utilities with user groups to monitor quality and responsiveness. The trustees are modifying their governance processes to enable board members to spend more time on critical new directions and major problems and less on routine administrative decisions. The legislature created strong local advisory boards in 1997 to democratize decision making further while it affirmed the authority and responsibility of the trustees and the system chancellor. The intent of these changes has been to enable campus presidents to exercise greater freedom while holding them responsible for addressing prominent regional and state needs, notably economic development. The system and the board have accepted the challenge of demonstrating that a system that is simultaneously decentralized and focused on state priorities offers a better alternative than either no-holds-barred competition or authoritarian control.

Assert Leadership on Top Public Priorities

For all the advantages of decentralizing authority, there are times when working together under enlightened and authoritative leadership presents a better option. As Mingle and Epper point out in Chapter Two, getting the most out of expensive new communications technology often requires decisive central decision making. The same holds true when it comes to uniting a collection of institutions in the cause of state economic development, seeking public funding, passing a referendum, and communicating with the public about the benefits of higher education.

Grant Citizen Boards the Authority to Act

These recommendations will be nearly impossible to implement unless lay boards receive discretionary powers at least approaching that of those who govern private institutions. Ingram in Chapter Seven suggests that public boards be granted the authority to set tuition rates and institutional financial aid, control their own budgets, manage and invest funds, and be allowed sufficient dispensation from open meeting laws to engage in candid discussions of critical issues. None of this is to say governors or legislators should not set high expectations for the deliverables of public institutions. But once these goals are identified in dialogue with trustees and academic leaders, then political leaders should step aside and allow the trustees to govern free of intrusion.

Conclusion

This book began with Robert Michels's declaration, "Who says organization, says oligarchy." The ensuing chapters suggest it ain't necessarily so. Preserving the value of independent centers of learning and discourse called colleges and universities, achieving greater responsiveness to the needs of student-consumers for high-quality programs, and ensuring that the public agenda is addressed lie in part in creating a new balance between freedom and oversight.

The chapter authors agree that the pendulum swing, which has increasingly shifted power from the campus to central boards or state bureaucracies, needs to be reversed. They concur that the challenges facing higher education, and indeed the country as a whole, are too many and too complex for top-down, centralized, and bureaucratic methods to work in bringing about needed change.

It is important to emphasize, however, that these apostles of reform do not advocate the wholesale privatization of public higher education. With differences of emphasis and terminology, each author makes the case for a redesigned but strong relationship between the campus and the state. A few examples illustrate this common ground. Callan and his associates describe this new relationship as a federal model with great latitude for campus decision making, but with clear leadership on judiciously selected issues from a board representing the public interest. Distinguishing between procedural autonomy, or the broad responsibility over financial management, academic policies, and fundraising, and substantive autonomy referring to authority over mission and fundamental questions of access, Berdahl recommends bestowing the former on the institution and the latter on state authorities. In championing greater discretion to lead for university presidents, Shaw calls for both a free-market environment for action and clear indicators for accountability. I describe the new relationship within systems of higher education as one that frees up universities and their leaders to exercise their entrepreneurial talents, but looks to the collective leadership to ensure scale economies on common services and attention to compelling public priorities. The conclusion would seem to be that it is not time to sever the relationship between the campus and the state but to retune the "suitably sensitive mechanisms" (Berdahl, 1971, p. 9) that link the two together.

References

Preface

Berdahl, R. *Statewide Coordination of Higher Education*. Washington, D.C.: American Council on Education, 1971.

MacTaggart, T., and Associates. *Restructuring Higher Education: What Works and What Doesn't in Reorganizing Governing Systems*. San Francisco: Jossey-Bass, 1996.

Newman, F. *Choosing Quality: Reducing Conflict Between the State and the University*. Denver: Education Commission of the States, 1987.

Slaughter, S., and Leslie, L. *Academic Capitalism: Politics, Policies, and the Entrepreneurial University*. Baltimore, Md.: Johns Hopkins University Press, 1997.

Chapter One

Bennis, W. *Why Leaders Can't Lead: The Unconscious Conspiracy Continues*. San Francisco: Jossey-Bass, 1989.

Berdahl, R. *Statewide Coordination of Higher Education*. Washington, D.C.: American Council on Education, 1971.

Berdahl, R., and Schmidtlein, F. "Restructuring and Its Aftermath: Maryland." In T. MacTaggart and Associates, *Restructuring Higher Education: What Works and What Doesn't in Reorganizing Governing Systems*. San Francisco: Jossey-Bass, 1996.

Berger, J. "A School Board Eager for Change: Where Decentralization Began, Hope for Albany's New Plan." *New York Times*, Dec. 20, 1996, p. B3.

Callan, P. "The Gauntlet for Multicampus Systems." *Trusteeship*, 1994, *2*(3), 16–19.

Commission on the Academic Presidency. *Renewing the Academic Presidency: Stronger Leadership for Tougher Times*. Washington, D.C.: Association of Governing Boards of Colleges and Universities, 1996.

DeBiaggio, J. A., Haaland, G. A., and Sample, S. B. "Confessions of a Public University Refugee." *Trusteeship,* 1996, *4*(3), 6–9.

Dhiratayakinant, K. *Privatization: An Analysis of the Concept and Its Implementation in Thailand.* Bangkok: Thailand Development Research Institute Foundation, 1989.

Eaton, J. S. "Privatizing American Education II: This Time It's Higher Education." *Council Comments,* no. 6. New York: Council for Aid to Education, 1994.

Finn, C. "Reforming Education: A Whole New World." *First Things,* May 1997, pp. 33–38.

Fisher, J. "The Failure of Statewide Coordination." *Chronicle of Higher Education,* June 16, 1995, p. A48.

Gade, M. *Systems: What Works? A Study of "Good Ideas" from Four Systems of Higher Education in the U.S.* Washington, D.C.: Association of Governing Boards of Universities and Colleges, 1993.

Gerson, M. (ed.). *The Essential Neoconservative Reader.* Reading, Mass.: Addison-Wesley, 1996.

Kahn, A. *The Economics of Regulation: Principles and Institutions.* Cambridge, Mass.: MIT Press, 1995. (Originally published 1970.)

Kerr, C., and Gade, M. L. *The Guardians: What They Do and How Well They Do It.* Washington, D.C.: Association of Governing Boards of Universities and Colleges, 1989.

Kristol, I. "Human Nature and Social Reform." In M. Gerson (ed.), *The Essential Neoconservative Reader.* Reading, Mass.: Addison-Wesley, 1996.

Kuttner, R. *Everything for Sale: The Virtues and Limits of Markets.* New York: Knopf, 1997.

Langenberg, D. "Why a System? Understanding the Costs and Benefits of Joining Together." *Change,* Mar.–Apr. 1994, pp. 3–4.

MacTaggart, T. "Restructuring and the Failure of Reform." In T. MacTaggart and Associates, *Restructuring Higher Education: What Works and What Doesn't in Reorganizing Governing Systems.* San Francisco: Jossey-Bass, 1996.

Martin, J., and Associates. *Merging Colleges for Mutual Growth: A New Strategy for Academic Managers.* Baltimore, Md.: Johns Hopkins University Press, 1994.

McGuinness, A. C., Jr. "The Changing Structures of State Higher Education Leadership." In A. C. McGuinness, Jr., R. Epper, and S. Arredondo (eds.), *State Postsecondary Education Structures Handbook: State Coordinating and Governing Boards.* Denver: Education Commission of the States, 1994.

McGuinness, A. C., Jr. "A Model for Successful Restructuring." In T. MacTaggart and Associates, *Restructuring Higher Education: What Works and What Doesn't in Reorganizing Governing Systems.* San Francisco: Jossey-Bass, 1996.

Michels, R. *Political Parties.* New York: Dover, 1959. (Originally published 1915.)

Neuhaus, J., and Berger, P. *To Empower People: The Role of Mediating Structures in Public Policy.* Washington, D.C.: American Enterprise Institute, 1976.

Newman, F. *Choosing Quality: Reducing Conflict Between the State and the University.* Denver: Education Commission of the States, 1987.

Osborne, D., and Gaebler, T. *Reinventing Government: How the Entrepreneurial Spirit Is Transforming the Public Sector.* Reading, Mass.: Addison-Wesley, 1992.

"Over-Regulating America." *Economist,* July 27, 1996, pp. 19–21.

Wilson, J. Q. *Bureaucracy: What Government Agencies Do and Why They Do It.* New York: Basic Books, 1989.

Wilson, J. Q. "Foreword." In M. Gerson (ed.), *The Essential Neoconservative Reader.* Reading, Mass.: Addison-Wesley, 1996.

Chapter Two

Ashworth, K. H. "Virtual Universities Could Produce Only Virtual Learning." *Chronicle of Higher Education,* Sept. 6, 1996, p. A88.

Auletta, K. "Fourteen Truisms for the Communications Revolution." *Media Studies Journal,* 1996, *10*(2/3), 28–38.

Babson College Reengineering Design Team. *The Executive Summary: A Blueprint for Enhanced Customer Service Through Information Technology Enablement.* Babson Park, Mass.: Babson College, 1994.

Baltzer, J., and Slobodzian, K. "Electronically Providing Instructional Support Services for the Distance Learner." Paper presented at the annual meeting of CAUSE, San Francisco, Dec. 1996.

California State University. *Status Report on the Integrated Technology Strategies Initiative.* Long Beach: California State University, Mar. 1996.

Colorado Commission on Higher Education. *Handout: Information Technology and Distance Education Surveys.* Denver: Colorado Commission on Higher Education, June 1996.

Cooper, C. [ccooper@unm.edu]. "Responses on Distance Learning Instruction-Service Areas." In SHEEO Academic Officers Listserv. [SHEEO-academic@osshe.edu]. June 3, 1996.

Daniel, J. S. *Mega-Universities and Knowledge Media: Technology Strategies for Higher Education.* London: Kogan Page, 1996.

Davis, S. M., and Botkin, J. W., *The Monster Under the Bed: How Business Is Mastering the Opportunity of Knowledge for Profit.* New York: Simon & Schuster, 1994.

Doucette, D. S., and others. "Surveying Technology's New Landscape." *Trusteeship,* 1996 (special issue), pp. 10–15.

Epper, R. M. "Coordination and Competition in Postsecondary Distance Education: A Comparative Case Study of Statewide Policies." Unpublished doctoral dissertation, College of Education, University of Denver, 1996.

Gilbert, S. W. "Making the Most of a Slow Revolution." *Change,* 1996, *28*(2), 10–23.

Gillespie, R. *A Report on Colorado Network Development to the Colorado Commission on Higher Education.* Bellevue, Wash.: Robert Gillespie Associates, 1996.

Green, K. C. *Campus Computing 1996.* Encino, Calif.: Campus Computing, 1996.

Gurbaxani, V., and Whang, S. "The Impact of Information Systems on Organizations and Markets." *Communications of the ACM,* 1991, *34*(1), 59–73.

Gwinn, D. G., and Lonabocker, L. (eds.). *Breakthrough Systems: Student Access and Registration.* Washington, D.C.: American Association of Collegiate Registrars and Admissions Officers, 1996.

Hezel Associates and State Higher Education Executive Officers (SHEEO). *Statewide Funding of Educational Technology for Higher Education.* Syracuse, N.Y.: Hezel Associates, 1997.

Hornback, R. "Electronic Commerce in the 21st Century." *Journal of Systems Management,* 1995, *46*(3), 28–33.

Indiana Commission for Higher Education. "Policy for Authorizing New Campuses and Off-Campus Sites." (As approved by the Commission for Higher Education on Oct. 11, 1996). Indianapolis: Indiana Commission for Higher Education, 1996.

Lucas, H. C., Jr. *The T-Form Organization: Using Technology to Design Organizations for the 21st Century.* San Francisco: Jossey-Bass, 1996.

Lucas, H. C., Jr., and Baroudi, J. "The Role of Information Technology in Organizational Design." *Journal of Management Information Systems,* 1994, *10*(4), 9–23.

Oberlin, J. "The Financial Mythology of Information Technology." Paper presented at the annual meeting of Educom, Philadelphia, Oct. 1996.

Oklahoma State Regents for Higher Education. *OneNet: Business Plan for Expansion and Upgrade.* Oklahoma City: Oklahoma State Regents for Higher Education, Aug. 1995.

Porter, M. E. *Competitive Strategy: Techniques for Analyzing Industries and Competitors.* New York: Free Press, 1980.

Record, S. "A Library for the Ages." *Multiversity* (IBM Magazine for Colleges and Universities), Winter 1996, pp. 4–7.

State Higher Education Executive Officers (SHEEO). *SHEEO/FIPSE Project Final Report: Gaining State Commitment to a Redesigned Delivery System.* Denver: State Higher Education Executive Officers, 1996.

Twigg, C. A. *Academic Productivity: The Case for Instructional Software.* Report from the Broadmoor Roundtable, Colorado Springs, Colo., July 24–25, 1996. Washington, D.C.: Educom, 1996.

Weick, K. E. "Educational Organizations as Loosely Coupled Systems." *Administrative Science Quarterly,* 1976, *21*(1), 1–19.

Western Governors Association. *Western Governors University: A Proposed Implementation Plan.* Denver: Western Governors Association, June 1996.

Witherspoon, J. P. *Distance Education: A Planner's Casebook.* Boulder, Colo.: Western Interstate Commission for Higher Education, July 1996.

Chapter Three

DeBiaggio, J. A., Haaland, G. A., and Sample, S. B. "Confessions of a Public University Refugee." *Trusteeship,* 1996, *4*(3), 6–9.

Wilson, J. Q. *Bureaucracy: What Government Agencies Do and Why They Do It.* New York: Basic Books, 1989.

Chapter Four

Berdahl, R. *Statewide Coordination of Higher Education.* Washington, D.C.: American Council on Education, 1971.

Berdahl, R., and Schmidtlein, F. "Restructuring and Its Aftermath: Maryland." In T. MacTaggart and Associates, *Restructuring Higher Education: What Works and What Doesn't in Reorganizing Governing Systems.* San Francisco: Jossey-Bass, 1996.

Fausz, J. *Monument School of the People, a Sesquicentennial History of St. Mary's College of Maryland, 1840–1990.* St. Mary's City: St. Mary's College of Maryland, 1990.

Lewis, E. "Metamorphosis of a Public College." *Trusteeship,* 1994, *2*(5), 20–25.

Maryland Higher Education Commission. *General Fund History.* Annapolis: Maryland Higher Education Commission, Apr. 1996.

Maryland House of Delegates. House Bill 1327. 1992.

Middle States Association of Colleges and Schools, Evaluation Team. *Report to the Faculty, Administration, Trustees, Staff and Students of St. Mary's College of Maryland.* Philadelphia: Middle States Association of Colleges and Schools, Oct. 1995.

Reaccreditation Self-Study Committee. *Report of a Reaccreditation Self-Study Committee.* St. Mary's City: St. Mary's College of Maryland, Sept. 1995.

Chapter Five

Advisory Panel on Higher Education Restructuring. *Report of the Governors Advisory Panel on Higher Education Restructuring.* Trenton, N.J.: Advisory Panel on Higher Education Restructuring, May 5, 1994.

Education Commission of the States. *Restructuring State Roles in Higher Education, A Case Study of the New Jersey Higher Education Restructuring Act.* Denver, Colo.: Education Commission of the States, Dec. 1995.

Greer, D. G., and Shelly, P. R. "A State of Change." *Trusteeship,* 1995, *3*(4), 16.

Hollander, T. E. "Coordinating Boards Under Attack." *Chronicle of Higher Education,* Apr. 20, 1994, pp. B2–B4.

Millett, J. D. *Conflict in Higher Education: State Government Coordination Versus Institutional Independence.* San Francisco: Jossey-Bass, 1984.

New Jersey Commission on Higher Education and the New Jersey Presidents' Council. *The Restructuring of New Jersey Higher Education.* Trenton, N.J.: New Jersey Commission on Higher Education and the New Jersey Presidents' Council, May 31, 1996.

New Jersey State College Governing Boards Association. Ad Hoc Committee on State College Self-Governance. *Self-Governance and Accountability: A Report on the Implementation of the State College Autonomy Laws, 1986–1990.* Trenton, N.J.: New Jersey State College Governing Boards Association, June 1991.

New Jersey State College Governing Boards Association. *New Jerseyans Solving New Jersey's Problems: An Agenda for Investing in the State Colleges.* Staff Paper 93–01. Trenton, N.J.: New Jersey State College Governing Boards Association, Nov. 1993.

New Jersey State College Governing Boards Association. *State College/University Sourcebook: 1996 Edition.* Trenton, N.J. New Jersey State College Governing Boards Association, Apr. 1996.

New Jersey State College Governing Boards Association. *GBA Staff Report on Restructuring.* Trenton, N.J.: New Jersey State College Governing Boards Association, June 1996.

Schick, E. B., Novak, R. J., Norton, J. A., and Elam, H. G. *Shared Visions of Public Higher Education Governance: Structures and Leadership Styles That Work.* Washington, D.C.: American Association of State Colleges and Universities, with support from the American Council on Education, 1992.

Chapter Six

Adelman, C. *Tourists in Our Own Land: Cultural Literacies and the College Curriculum.* Washington, D.C.: Office of Educational Research and Improvement, U.S. Department of Education, Oct. 1992.

Atwell, R. H. "Financial Prospects for Higher Education." *Policy Perspectives,* Sept. 1992, *4*(3), 5B

Barr, R. T., and Tagg, J. "From Teaching to Learning—A New Paradigm for Undergraduate Education." *Change,* Nov.–Dec. 1995, pp. 13–21.

Barton, P. E., and Lapointe, A. *Learning by Degrees: Indicators of Performance in Higher Education.* Princeton, N.J.: Educational Testing Service, 1995.

Bok, D. *Universities and the Future of America.* Durham, N.C.: Duke University Press, 1990.

Breneman, D., Estrada, L., and Hayward, G. *Tidal Wave II: An Evaluation of Enrollment Projections for California Higher Education.* San Jose: California Higher Education Policy Center, 1995.

Carnegie Foundation for the Advancement of Teaching. *The States and Higher Education.* San Francisco: Jossey-Bass, 1976.

Drucker, P. F. *Post Capitalist Society.* New York: Harper Business, 1993.

Gold, S., and Ritchie, S. *State Spending Patterns in the 1990s.* Albany, N.Y.: Center for the Study of the States, 1995.

Handy, C. "Balancing Corporate Power: A New Federalist Paper." *Harvard Business Review,* 1992, *70*(6), 59–72.

Handy, C. *The Age of Paradox.* Boston: Harvard Business School Press, 1994.

Harvey, J., and Immerwahr, J. *The Fragile Coalition: Public Support for Higher Education in the 1990s.* Washington, D.C.: American Council on Education, 1995.

Heifetz, R. A. *Leadership Without Easy Answers.* Cambridge, Mass.: Belknap Press, 1994.

"Higher Education." *State Policy Reports,* 1995, *14*(1), 13–16.

Immerwahr, J. *Preserving the Higher Education Legacy: A Conversation with California Leaders.* San Jose: California Higher Education Policy Center, 1995.

Immerwahr, J., and Farkas, S. *The Closing Gateway: Californians Consider Their Higher Educational System.* San Jose: California Higher Education Policy Center, 1993.

Jacobs, J. "Student Fee Politics." *Sacramento Bee,* Jan. 16, 1996.

Johnstone, D. B. "Enhancing the Productivity of Learning." *AAHE Bulletin,* Dec. 1993, pp. 3–5.

Kerr, C. *The Great Transformation in Higher Education, 1960–1980.* Albany: State University of New York Press, 1991.

Kerr, C. *The Uses of the University.* (4th ed.) Cambridge, Mass.: Harvard University Press, 1995.

Marshall, R., and Tucker, M. *Thinking for a Living.* New York: Basic Books, 1992.

McMahon, E. M. "Lessons from the East: The Reinvention of Public Higher Education in New Jersey." Unpublished paper prepared for the

National Advisory Committee on Governance, California Higher Education Policy Center, San Jose, Calif., Jan. 1996.

Novak, R. J. "Methods, Objectives, and Consequences of Restructuring." In T. MacTaggart and Associates, *Restructuring Higher Education: What Works and What Doesn't in Reorganizing Governing Systems.* San Francisco: Jossey-Bass, 1996.

President's Council of Advisors on Science and Technology (PCAST). *Renewing the Promise: Research Intensive Universities and the Nation.* Washington, D.C.: Executive Office of the President, 1992.

RAND. *Does California's Future Bode Ill for Education?* Santa Monica, Calif.: RAND Institute of Education and Training, Jan. 1996.

Reich, R. B. "Introduction." In R. B. Reich, *The Power of Public Ideas.* Cambridge: Harvard University Press, 1988.

Richardson, R. C., Jr. "Illinois: An Interpretive Synthesis." Unpublished paper prepared for the National Advisory Committee on Governance, California Higher Education Policy Center, San Jose, Calif., Jan. 1996.

Shick, E. B., Novak, R. J., Norton, J. A., and Elam, H. G. *Shared Visions of Public Higher Education Governance: Structures and Leadership Styles That Work.* Washington, D.C.: American Association of State Colleges and Universities, 1992.

Technology and Restructuring Roundtable. *Leveraged Learning: Technology's Role in Restructuring Higher Education.* Stanford, Calif.: Stanford Forum for Higher Education Futures, 1995.

Thurow, L. C. *The Future of Capitalism.* New York: Morrow, 1996.

Trombley, W. "Ambitious Reform Agenda." *CrossTalk,* Oct. 1995, pp. 1, 4–6.

Trombley, W. "Priorities, Quality, Productivity." *CrossTalk,* Jan. 1996, pp. 1, 4–5, 8.

Trow, M. "Reflections on Higher Education in 2005." Paper prepared for a seminar of the International Council of Educational Development, Williamsburg, Va., June 1993.

Wadsworth, D. "The New Public Landscape." *AAHE Bulletin,* June 1995.

Western Interstate Commission on Higher Education (WICHE), Teachers Insurance and Annuity Association (TIAA), College Board. *High School Graduates: Projections by State, 1992–2009.* Boulder, Colo.: Western Interstate Commission on Higher Education, Teachers Insurance and Annuity Association, College Board, 1993.

Wingspread Group on Higher Education. *An American Imperative: Higher Expectations for Higher Education.* Racine, Wis.: Johnson Foundation, 1993.

Chapter Seven

Association of Governing Boards of Universities and Colleges. *Recommendations for Improving Trustee Selection in Public Colleges and Universities.* Washington, D.C.: Association of Governing Boards of Universities and Colleges, 1980.

Commission on the Academic Presidency. *Renewing the Academic Presidency: Stronger Leadership for Tougher Times.* Washington, D.C.: Association of Governing Boards of Universities and Colleges, 1996.

Hodgkinson, H. L. "The New Demography." In R. T. Ingram and Associates, *Governing Public Colleges and Universities: A Handbook for Trustees, Chief Executives, and Other Campus Leaders.* San Francisco: Jossey-Bass, 1993.

Lewis, E. T., Muller, S., and Aery, S. R. "Metamorphosis of a Public College." *Trusteeship,* 1994, *2*(5), 20–25.

McDonald, J. G. *Changing State Policies to Strengthen Public University and College Trustee Selection and Education.* AGB Public Policy Paper No. 95–2. Washington, D.C.: Association of Governing Boards of Universities and Colleges, 1995.

Ruppert, S. S. *The Politics of Remedy: State Legislative Views on Higher Education.* Washington, D.C.: National Education Association, 1996.

St. Mary's College of Maryland. *Report of a Special Board Committee.* (Unpublished.) St. Mary's College of Maryland, Nov. 10, 1992.

Chapter Eight

Bauer v. State Board of Agriculture, 164 Mich. 415, 418–419, 129 N.W. 713 (1911).

Board of Regents of the University of Michigan v. Auditor General, 167 Mich. 444, 450, 132, N.W. 1037 (1911).

Board of Regents of the University of Michigan v. State of Michigan, 166 Mich. App. (1988).

Chambers, M. M. *Voluntary Statewide Coordination in Public Higher Education.* Ann Arbor: University of Michigan, 1961.

Cole, K. "U-M Broke Law in Presidential Search, Court Rules. Decision: Open Meetings Act Violated." *Detroit News,* Sept. 29, 1993.

Cudlip, W. B. *The University of Michigan: Its Legal Profile.* Ann Arbor: University of Michigan, 1969.

Drake v. Regents of the University of Michigan, 4 Mich. 98 (1856).

Gill, J. I. "Higher Education and State Government in Michigan: A Historical and Organizational Analysis of the Relationship from 1950 to 1971." Unpublished doctoral dissertation, University of Michigan, 1987.

Glenny, L. A., and Dalglish, T. K. *Public Universities, State Agencies, and the Law: Constitutional Autonomy in Decline.* Berkeley: Center for Research and Development in Higher Education, University of California, 1973.

Governor's Commission on the Future of Higher Education in Michigan. *An Overview of Formula Funding in Higher Education.* Lansing: Governor's Commission on the Future of Higher Education in Michigan, 1984a.

Governor's Commission on the Future of Higher Education in Michigan. *Previous Michigan Higher Education Commissions.* Lansing: Governor's Commission on the Future of Higher Education in Michigan, 1984b.

Hearn, J., and Griswold, C. "State-Level Centralization and Policy Innovation in U.S. Postsecondary Education." *Educational Evaluation and Policy Analysis,* 1994, *16*(2), 161–190.

Hines, E. R. *Appropriations: State Tax Funds for Operating Expenses of Higher Education, 1995–1996.* Washington, D.C.: National Association of State Universities and Land-Grant Colleges, 1996a.

Hines, E. R. *State Higher Education Appropriations: 1991–92—1995–96.* Denver: State Higher Education Executive Officers Association, 1996b.

Hoover, R. "U-M Spends $530,197 on Search for New President." *Detroit News,* Feb. 6, 1997.

Laird, D. "The Regents of the University of Michigan and the Legislature of the State: 1920–1950." Unpublished doctoral dissertation, University of Michigan, 1972.

McGuinness, A. C., Jr. *State Postsecondary Education Structures Handbook: State Coordinating and Governing Boards.* Denver: Education Commission of the States, 1994.

Posthumus, D. "Higher Education Has Never Meant More." *Detroit News,* Feb. 14, 1995.

Regents of the University of Michigan v. *State of Michigan,* 47 Mich. App. 23 (1973).

Regents of the University of Michigan v. *State of Michigan,* 395 Mich. 52, 65, 235 N.W. 2d 1 (1975).

Schmidt v. *Regents of the University of Michigan,* 62 Mich. App. 54 (1975).

Schwarz, J.J.H. "The Role of the State in Higher Education: An Historical Perspective." Unpublished manuscript, 1994.

Sprik v. *Regents of the University of Michigan,* 390 Mich. 84 (1972).

State Board of Agriculture v. *Auditor General,* 180 Mich. 349 (1914).

State Board of Agriculture v. *Auditor General,* 226 Mich. 417 (1924).

Sterling v. *University of Michigan Regents,* 110 Mich. 369, 374, 68 N.W. 253 (1896).

U.S. Bureau of the Census. *Current Population Reports.* Washington, D.C., 1995.

U.S. Department of Education. *Digest of Education Statistics.* Washington, D.C., 1984.

U.S. Department of Education. *Digest of Education Statistics.* Washington, D.C., 1991.

U.S. Department of Education. *IPEDS Fall Enrollment Survey.* Washington, D.C., 1993.

U.S. Department of Education. *Digest of Education Statistics.* Washington, D.C., 1995.

Yniguez, J. *Report on State Programs Benefitting Independent Colleges and Their Students.* Washington, D.C.: National Institute of Independent Colleges and Universities, 1995.

Chapter Nine

Berdahl, R. *Statewide Coordination of Higher Education.* Washington, D.C.: American Council on Education, 1971.

Berdahl, R., and Schmidtlein, F. "Restructuring and Its Aftermath: Maryland." In T. MacTaggart and Associates, *Restructuring Higher Education: What Works and What Doesn't in Reorganizing Governing Systems.* San Francisco: Jossey-Bass, 1996.

California Higher Education Policy Center. *State Structures for the Governance of Higher Education: A Comparative Study.* San Jose: California Higher Education Policy Center, 1997.

Hines, E. R. *Appropriations: State Tax Funds for Operating Expenses of Higher Education, 1995–1996.* Washington, D.C.: National Association of State Universities and Land-Grant Colleges, 1996.

McGuinness, A. C., Jr. "A Model for Successful Restructuring." In T. MacTaggart and Associates, *Restructuring Higher Education: What Works and What Doesn't in Reorganizing Governing Systems.* San Francisco: Jossey-Bass, 1996.

Pew Higher Education Research Program. "The Lattice and the Ratchet." *Policy Perspectives,* 1990, *2*(4), 1–8.

Wilson, J. Q. *Bureaucracy: What Government Agencies Do and Why They Do It.* New York: Basic Books, 1989.

Index